THE MIRROR AND THE CROSS

Scotland and the Catholic Faith

by

GEORGE SCOTT-MONCRIEFF

LONDON

BURNS & OATES

NIHIL OBSTAT: PETER CONNOLLY, D.D., D.C.L.
CENSOR DEPUTATUS
IMPRIMATUR: ✠ GORDON J. GRAY
ARCHIEPISCOPUS S. ANDREAE ET EDIMBURGENSIS
DIE IX AUGUSTI MCMLX

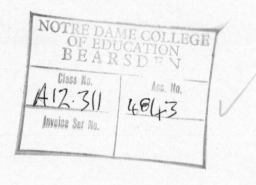
Made and printed in Great Britain by
Ditchling Press Ltd, Hassocks, Sussex,
and bound by Leighton-Straker Bookbinding Co. Ltd,
London, N.W.10, for
Burns and Oates Limited
28 Ashley Place, London, S.W.1

CONTENTS

Contents

ILLUSTRATIONS

Amongst many others, I am particularly indebted to Fr James Quinn, s.j., and to Fr Anthony Ross, o.p., for their help, guidance and encouragement while writing this book.

GEORGE SCOTT-MONCRIEFF

Edinburgh

Feast of St Thomas Aquinas, 1960.

PROLOGUE

THE mirror is one of half-a-dozen emblems regularly found on the earliest Pictish carved stones. There follows a phase in which the mirror and the other more or less pagan emblems are combined with a cross. Thereafter they disappear, and the stones are simply carved with the cross, sometimes richly ornamented or set against a background of men and beasts. There is some dispute as to the precise significance of these earlier emblems: but one might say that a mirror implies a man's ability to look at himself, the beginning perhaps of his deliberate self-consciousness.

History too is a manner of looking at ourselves. But there is more room for divergence in what we see in the mirror of history: opinions, our own and other people's, affect our vision.

Every opinion has its bias. We see history through our predilections, and measure it by particular scales of value. Scottish history has long been chiefly written with a Protestant bias, sometimes a very marked one. Generally it has come to be accepted as a somewhat shaky but beneficent progression culminating in Protestant reform and the English union. Everything that contributed, or might be made to seem to contribute, to this apotheosis represented the forces of good, everything else was either downright betrayal or, if room had to be made for it, a romantic side-issue.

But to bring the story of a country to any such artificial termination is only to attempt to trim the flowing robe of history into a suit tailored to fit a dummy figure. This particular attempt does not wear so well in the upheaved world of the mid-twentieth century as it did when the millennium seemed almost within the grasp of a dominant Britain, and we are coming to look at our country's past again without the imposition of a conclusion that can no longer claim the conviction that it could in the days of Macaulay and his Scottish disciples.

What we know as history is a cumulative deduction from the lives of many men, but we should never forget that, save in the case of a few megalomaniacs, they were not primarily concerned to contribute to that story in their individual lives: the purpose of each individual is simpler and more personal, and each man takes his own true history to the grave with him. At its worst it is a reversion to the brute: at its best it becomes focused in realizing his relationship with God. In this most can agree: disagreement starts with the nature of the relationship, and, of course, with ideas on the nature of God himself.

Yet in Scotland, as elsewhere, conflicting attitudes have changed greatly and wholesomely since the first days of Protestantism. Protestants whose leaders were once bitterly anxious that they should regard Rome as the implacable enemy of Christ, generally now accept Catholics as making a different, if misguided, approach to him. To the Catholic likewise Protestants are no longer to be seen as of necessity in bad faith, but, sharing the same Redeemer and the same baptism, as fellow-travellers with himself, although deprived by some historical accident of the fullness of the faith they share.

"No man is an island", and the Scottish Catholic cannot afford to feel what it was once, in penal times and while the memory of them remained strong, very hard for him not to feel—namely, cut off from his own countrymen, never fully sharing either their achievement or their failure. There are today twice as many Catholics in Scotland as there were before the Reformation, and if they represent only a minority of the total population it is a substantial one. Through all the fifteen hundred years that have passed since the first missionaries established it in our country, there have always been in Scotland those in full communion with the Church of Rome, and priests, even if at times they were reduced to a bare half-dozen, to bring them her sacraments. Moreover, those whom the failure of priest and layfolk alike separated from the whole faith, have still shared much of it, often heroically. The Scottish convert of today does not feel that he is repudiating the faith of his immediate forebears: rather he is likely to feel a profound gratitude and respect for what they maintained and for an example and teaching that has led him full circle to the faith as it was held intact for the first thousand years of Christianity in Scotland. Yet we have still to see the last four hundred years not so much as a break in that tradition as somehow a continuing part of it: if there has been sorrow and loss, there has been much good that must be seen as such. We may only dimly understand the forces that made for separation amongst those who recognize in Christ the Son of God, but the gulf must never be allowed to pervert us again into an apprehensive narrowness. About ideas it is folly to be slack and casual, as though there were no knowable truth: but the alternative is not a position of exclusive righteousness. True confidence opens the heart and increases understanding.

Our view of history is always limited; the past is subject to misrepresentation, the present to prejudice, the foreseeable future is only speculation. Truth is not the fruit of our insufficiently informed opinions but abides outside them. While the Reformers of 1560 could claim justice for their disgust with the failure of Churchmen to practise what they preached, they made the disastrous error of wishing to change not only the practice but also the precepts, and so obscured revealed religion in a cloud of opinion whose transience has been manifest in subsequent change, schism and confusion. Her leaders humbled and brought low, the Church herself reduced in Scotland to a minority creed, she has brought forth in these four hundred years new leaders, men of zealous and pure lives, and, in retaining her creed intact, her teaching has been enriched by the common growth in human knowledge. By the end of the eighteenth century all the barricades of propaganda could not prevent Robert Burns from seeing in John Geddes, a Catholic bishop, the finest Christian cleric he had ever met.

But prejudice goes deep and lives long. The Church, reinforced by Irish immigration in the last century, is even accused of being "un-Scottish", an alien intrusion. Yet although the first Scottish missionary of whom we have any record was a native Pict, it was missionaries from Ireland who originally consolidated our country, and much of England and Wales, in Christianity, and the fullness of their faith was never entirely lost to Scotland but survived even a relentless persecution. It could be more convincingly argued that our Protestantism was an alien intrusion, effectively established as it was to a Genevan model by the political imperialism of England. Similarly, Catholicism comes under fire for being the faith of many amongst the more improvident and criminal. This is scarcely to appreciate the legacy bequeathed by the slumdom and sweated labour of the days of reckless industrial development that found its cheap labour largely amongst an uprooted and destitute Irish peasantry. Moreover, Christ came to save sinners, and while detesting the sin the Church exists to minister to those who commit it, not, as tended to be done by orthodox Calvinism, rejecting them as predestined to damnation.

The narrow and nervous faith that we describe as puritanical is certainly not confined to Protestantism. It tends to be a defence developed in times of oppression and persecution, and as such, even although its manifestations may often be pathetic and deleterious to a true spirituality, we should not judge it too harshly (too puritanically!), since the alternative to such defence might only be an abject surrender. But throughout her long history the Church has again and again condemned efforts to rarefy faith to the exclusion of the good things of God's creation, efforts made in a belief most liable to gain currency in hard times, the belief that the world itself is evil and redemption confined to the spirit. She has always seen men as a whole, body and spirit; God to be glorified in all his creation, the arts and the sciences, the beauty of nature and of human love. She has seen in Manicheism, Calvinism, Jansenism, anxious attempts to preserve faith by confining it, putting a human limit to the vastness of divine charity. She has pointed the answer in canonizing men and women who not only overcame evil but also overcame the fear of evil, and whose sufferings never quenched the gaiety of their goodness.

Today we hope more fervently than ever for Christian unity. We have had appalling reminders of the savagery that is always ready to break out in man when he repudiates his Creator. We know, or we have no excuse for not knowing, that material gains and intellectual enlightenment are not necessarily to our advantage, but dependent for their good upon the charity that men can only learn in humility before God.

The ensuing pages are an effort to present in brief outline something of the historical background of his faith to the Scottish Catholic, and to the non-Catholic some idea of how we who are members of the Church see our country's story in relation to that faith. We share a common heritage; our lives are bound up together in their needs, their successes and failures. Faith is a gift and in what measure and manner it is granted must always remain a mystery, but the dispersal of prejudice and the clarifying of human assessment are the desiderata of all honest men.

CHAPTER I

FOUNDATIONS

IN 1949 excavations brought back to light the cradle of Christianity in Scotland. At the east end of the ruins of the priory church built at Whithorn in 1150 were unearthed part of the walls, still daubed with white lime, of the little church, the *Candida Casa*, founded by St Ninian about the year 397.

The son of a Pictish chieftain of Galloway, Ninian seems to have been brought up a Christian under the Roman influence that held a tenuous sway in the south of Scotland. Tradition has it that he went to Rome and that Pope Damasus supervised his studies for the priesthood. It is said he spent fifteen years in Rome. As they were contemporaries, we have a clear picture in the *Confessions* of St Augustine of the environment that Ninian would find there: a world exemplifying much of the best and the worst of civilization, a decadence from which only Christianity offered spiritual redemption, superbly analysed in a book of a profundity and a breadth that make the discontent of the angry young men of the mid-twentieth century read like the graffiti of junior school-boys.

In Scotland it was a barbarian and simple people to whom Ninian returned, travelling by way of Tours where he spent some time at St Martin's monastery. Thus the semi-eremitical monasticism that St Martin had derived from the practice of the Desert Fathers of Egypt became the basis of the community founded at Whithorn. Nearby, on the coast at Glasserton, there is the cave which Ninian himself used as a hermitage, and the little peninsula called the Isle of Whithorn was perhaps the home of a community of monks living in separate cells. Yet, as an ordained bishop like St Martin himself, Ninian was occupied also in an active life, making missionary journeys to far parts of Scotland.

After his death, little is known of the community at Whithorn for over a century, when it emerges again as an important missionary school, training monks from Ireland and Wales. At about this times Gildas, a Briton from Strathclyde, wrote a fierce polemic, *De Excidio Britanniae*, in which he contrasted the ideal of the Christian life with the prevailing lukewarm practice of it, and did much to inspire the establishing of a monasticism that, receiving its most enthusiastic response in Ireland, became the great force in Celtic Christianity. If at first the Irish were borrowers from Pict and Briton (St Patrick himself was not an Irishman, but a Briton, perhaps from Strathclyde), the time soon came when St Columba was to head a long line of missionaries who confirmed Scotland in the Christian faith, and effectively laid the foundations of her history as a nation.

Certain historical characters stake exceptional claim upon our attention. Their names acquire the quality of a legend that may even be quite remote from verifiable historical fact, and is generally at least somewhat distorted, or over-simplified for easy consumption. So St Columba has come to figure in Scottish minds rather as a benign visionary practising the gentler virtues in the misty obscurity of Iona. The force, the scale and achievement of the man are somehow minimized in the apocryphal legend of his being expelled for a hot-headed youthful indiscretion and seeking exile out of sight of Ireland.

In fact Columba was a man of forty-two when he came to Iona in the year 563: a man who had already completed more than a normal life's work in his native Ireland, founding a series of major monasteries, carrying weight in civil affairs, yet spending much time in study, composing poetry in Latin and in Gaelic and making three hundred careful transcriptions of the Gospels and the Psalms. He came to what is now called Scotland for two reasons. Firstly, because of his desire to spread knowledge of Christ in parts predominantly pagan. Secondly, out of concern for the Irish colony, those Scots who had settled along the coast of Argyll and in the adjacent islands. The ruler of these immigrant Scots in Dalriada was of Columba's own blood-royal, and in 563 he and his people were in danger of being driven out of the country by their most powerful neighbours, the Northern Picts. Columba founded his monastery in Iona because it was isolated yet central, and he must surely have been drawn by the particular beauty of the island.

Scotland at this time was divided into six kingdoms: the Scots of Dalriada, the Northern Picts, the Southern Picts, Britons of Strathclyde, with an Anglic settlement in Lothian and a Pictish outpost in Galloway. The most powerful of its rulers was Brude, King of the Northern Picts. Columba travelled to Inverness where he converted Brude to Christianity, and made peace between him and the Scots. Some years later he visited Ireland to establish the independence of Dalriada from Irish superiority. By these achievements Columba may fairly be said to have shaped the future of Scotland. Yet his main work was as a Christian missionary, and here again he sowed seeds that were to bear fruit far beyond the range of his own immediate activities. Monks from Iona were later to convert the North of England, and, at the end of the Dark Ages, they and the monks of Columba's monasteries in Ireland were to contribute to the revival of Christianity on the continent of Europe itself.

Although he spent most of his time in his monastery it served also as the base from which Columba travelled on missions to further islands and into the different territories of the Scottish mainland. Place-names scattered wide over the country recall the journeys and religious foundations made by Columba and his followers. In the Isle of Skye, in Tiree and Canna, across the Minch in Lewis, Bernera, Benbecula, the Uists; in Oransay, Mull, Islay, and remote St Kilda; along the shores of mainland Dalriada, at Ardchattan, Morvern, Kintyre; into the Brythonic territories of Strathclyde, at Kilmacolm in Renfrew, Largs in Ayrshire, and into the Pictish Kingdom of Galloway. Amongst the Northern Picts monasteries or churches were founded in Banffshire and Aberdeenshire, at Kingussie in Inverness-shire, in Caithness and Sutherland, and over the sea in the Orkney islands of Hoy and Sanday. In the territory of the Southern Picts Dunkeld was the most important foundation, later the seat of a diocese and for a short time the ecclesiastical capital of Scotland.

B

The rule of life of the Columban community, derived through Whithorn and Tours, developed as part of the general monastic movement of the time. The monks had separate huts—at Tours they had caves—although, outside their hours of solitude, they lived a communal life. Each cell had its straw mattress and pillow. They wore habits, cowl and tunic, of undyed wool, with a cloak for protection in rough weather. Saturday was regarded like the Jewish Sabbath as a day of rest: not in the curious fashion in which, a thousand years later, Scottish Presbyterians came to call Sunday the Sabbath, making it a day of enforced and rather melancholy restraint, but as preparation, after the intensive work of the week, for the celebration of Sunday's ritual. There were lay-brothers whose work was domestic and agricultural. The ordained monks spent much of their time in study and calligraphy. Besides the Scriptures and lives of the saints, they knew the Latin works of the Classical authors. The Book of Kells is the product of one of Columba's monasteries and is evidence of the quality of their artistry. Hospitality was given an important place, and the monks studied the medicine of the time so that they could serve the sick as well as dispensing alms to the poor.

While he held matrimony in high honour, Columba and his monks accepted for themselves the ideal of chastity so that their union with God should be untrammelled. They renounced private property. "Be always naked", runs St Columba's Rule, "in imitation of Christ and according to the precepts of the Gospel." And the Rule exhorts:

A mind prepared for red martyrdom. A mind fortified and steadfast for white martyrdom. Forgiveness from the heart to everyone. Constant prayers for those who trouble thee. Follow almsgiving before all things. Take not of food until thou art hungry. The love of God with all thy heart and all thy strength. The love of thy neighbour as thyself. Abide in God's testaments throughout all times. Thy measure of prayer shall be until thy tears come; or thy measure of work of labour until thy tears come.

Although in St Columba's own day it was celebrated only on Sundays and holy days, the Eucharistic Sacrifice of the Mass was

the central act of worship, as it was for all the communities of the
Celtic churchmen. It was difficult, of course, to maintain an
adequate supply of wine. Most of it was imported from Marseilles,
and fragments of amphorae from the Mediterranean lands are
still occasionally found in the Scottish islands. Certain of the
monks, not Columba himself, were ordained bishops. As such,
they lived the ordinary communal life, but took precedence, when
present, in offering the Sacrifice, which otherwise might be
consecrated by a number of priests acting in common. Communion was received, usually in both kinds, not frequently, but
always by the whole community at Easter. Abbots of the Celtic
monasteries were generally appointed from amongst the kinsmen
of the founder-abbot, a practical enough procedure although one
that later led to abuse.

Considering he lived so long ago, at a time separated from the
present by many cataclysms that caused the loss of manuscript
and tradition, we know a great deal about Columba. He is the
subject of the very early biography written by St Adamnan before
700, unique in its day in Europe for its completeness. Adamnan
was himself an Abbot of Iona, and his life overlapped the lives of
those who had known Columba. Other early documents record
traditions that survived orally of the life of this man of vast vitality
and the most lively intelligence, a poet and a man of action, able
to arouse love and loyalty wherever he went. His memory
remained fresh and was revered even by those who, during the
dispute about the Celtic reckoning of Easter and form of tonsure,
were in disagreement with the monks of Iona. Long after, in the
eighteenth century, remembrance of Columba inspired Dr
Johnson to write the celebrated passage describing his visit to
Iona:

> We were now treading that illustrious island whence savage
> clans and roving barbarians derived the benefits of knowledge
> and the blessings of religion. . . . Far from me and from my
> friends be such frigid philosophy as may conduct us indifferent
> and unmoved over any ground which has been dignified by
> wisdom, bravery, or virtue. That man is little to be envied
> whose patriotism would not gain force upon the plain of

Marathon, or whose piety would not grow warmer among the ruins of Iona.

Since Dr Johnson's day scholarly research has endorsed everything that tradition held about the significance of Columba and his monks of Iona. Less informed was the special pleading made by some later divines of the reformed Churches to adopt him as an early "reformer" and to see the "Celtic Church" as a unit distinct from the main body of the Catholic Church. Although their arguments have long been discredited, something of their ideas still lingers amongst Scottish Protestants to confuse the popular picture of St Columba. Yet we may quote a Presbyterian minister, the Rev. J. C. MacNaught, who, in his authoritative study, *The Celtic Church and the See of Peter*, concludes unequivocally: "As the result of our investigations we have come to the conclusion that the ancient Celtic Church, so far from being independent of Rome in the sense of repudiating Papal Supremacy, was simply a part of the Catholic Church and with the whole Church acknowledged the Pope as its visible head." Of any relationship between the Reformers of the sixteenth century and St Columba, the same author says with equal clarity:

The Reformers, while they succeeded in abolishing some real abuses, destroyed also much of the edifice of faith and worship erected by SS. Ninian, Kentigern and Columba. They threw down the altars and substituted for them tables for the administration of the Lord's Supper. To them the Mass was something abhorrent, a blasphemous and idolatrous rite. If their doctrine was true, Columba every time he went up to the altar to celebrate "the pure mysteries of the sacred offering" committed the heinous sins of blasphemy and idolatry. If the Reformers were preachers of the pure Gospel, Columba assuredly was a perverter of the truth, who, had he been living in Scotland under the *régime* of John Knox, would have found himself liable to be put to death as a mass-priest.

Adamnan describes the death of Columba: the white farm horse that nuzzled its master as if knowing that he was going to die; the saint foretelling, "Upon this place, small though it be, and mean, not only the Kings of the Scots, with their peoples, but also the rulers of barbarous and foreign races, with the people subject to them, shall confer great and no common honour; by the Saints also even of other churches shall no common reverence be accorded to it." Then, as he lay with his head on his pillow of stone, his counsel to the monks gathered around him: "These my last words I commend to you, O my sons, that ye have mutual and unfeigned charity among yourselves, with peace; and if, according to the example of the holy Fathers, ye shall observe this, God, the Comforter of the good, will help you; and I, abiding with Him, will intercede for you; and not only will the necessaries of this present life be sufficiently supplied by Him, but the rewards of the good things of Eternity, prepared for those who keep His Divine Commandments, shall also be bestowed."

Before he died, in 597 at a time when the world about him may well have seemed a very peaceful place, Columba foretold the destruction of his monastery and the dispersal of its monks, but that the monks would return. Iona was to know another two hundred years of peace before vikings first raided the island in 795. A whole series of bloody raids was to follow during the next two centuries. On one occasion all the monks save one were murdered. Again and again the monks returned, rebuilt their church and cells, and carried on their mission. More peaceful times came after the defeat of the Danish vikings by their Norwegian rivals and the subsequent conversion to Christianity of the Norwegians.

But meanwhile the Irish Church to which Iona remained linked had suffered decline. In Scotland, as in Ireland, kings appointed lay abbots. Abbots themselves, lay and religious living in concubinage, settled their offspring in the possession of Church property. Riches that had been made possible by the civilizing influence of the earlier monks became a source of corruption for their successors. Iona itself seems rather to have become impoverished and undermanned until about the year 1074 when Queen Margaret restored and endowed the ancient monastery. Shortly after this, however, the island passed under the rule of the Norwegian king and the old Columban order of Iona came to an end with the death of the last of the abbots in

1099. Some fifty years later Irish monks were brought back, but the last phase really begins with the introduction of Benedictine monks from the south of Scotland by the Lord of the Isles about 1203. A nunnery was also founded, originally Benedictine but later Augustinian in its rule. For a short time, from about 1498, the Abbey Church became the Cathedral Church of the Diocese of the Isles. But a decline had set in, the buildings became dilapidated and appropriated by laymen, and then at last, just a thousand years after Columba first landed on Iona, the Reformation completed its desolation. Crosses and monuments were smashed, the great library was destroyed, although a handful of early manuscripts was rescued and taken to the Continent; church and conventual buildings wasted and decayed. For long enough the tombs of the Scottish, Irish and Norwegian kings who had had their bodies taken to the hallowed island for burial were left in dereliction. A greater respect for history has since brought belated preservation. The church itself was restored at the beginning of the twentieth century, and the monastic buildings of the Benedictine monks have lately been rebuilt for a Church of Scotland organization.

The Iona landscape remains beautiful in its scale and compactness. The sea turns an exquisite green as it runs across the white sand, or is stained purple above rocks and seaweed. Mountains and further islands lie watchfully over the waters. The skies can have a great lucidity, crossed by pageants of swift-moving clouds. This was the place of tranquillity of the man from Ireland who, more than any other single individual, shaped the destiny of Scotland.

Of course the directing of that destiny depended upon many others. Nor was Columba the first Christian missionary. But much of Scotland had never been converted, and even the communities reached by St Ninian's Pictish mission had largely returned to paganism before Columba's time. In coming as he did to the Dalriadic Scots when they were threatened with defeat at the hands of the Northern Picts, Columba brought the peace that established his own people in Scotland. This was no imperialism, for it was Columba again who negotiated the independence of the Scots colony from the rule of those in Ireland, and, as it were, made natives of them. Although the succeeding centuries were to see many changes and phases, with much of Scotland for a short time under the rule of Northumbria, and, for much longer, under the dominance of vikings from Denmark and Norway, it was a Scots king, Kenneth mac Alpin, under whom Picts and Scots were eventually united in the year 844. At first the line of Kenneth was known as the Kings of the Picts, later as Kings of Alba, but it eventually reverted to the title King of Scots. So when Columba crowned the Dalriadic King Aidan at Iona in the first Christian coronation ceremony in Britain, it was with the title that subsequently became that of the kingship of the whole country, and our very name derives from the achievement of the saint whose collateral descendants remain the royal house of Britain. Scots who were originally all Irishmen became the people of Caledonia, and their new land, with all its mixture of races, was called after them.

In later times heroic warriors, Malcom Canmore, Wallace and Bruce, took their part in welding the nation together; but warfare is at best primarily a matter of defence, and it is only in peace that countries can create what is worth defending. Columba's peaceful mission laid the foundations of our civilization, enlightening our forebears with values beyond immediate desires of gain or satisfaction. Nor were these values merely social, but a fruit of the supernatural life that was Columba's strength and devotion: and the greatest of his achievements lay in the realm of that Catholic Faith that is still held by a fair proportion of the people of Scotland, and informs, in varying degrees, the belief of the majority.

CHAPTER II

GROWTH

LIKE St Columba but unlike most of the other Celtic saints St Cuthbert has the advantage of an early biographer: in fact, he had two, one being the great historian Bede, and copies of their works were quickly distributed through Europe. Niceties of personality were not considered so important in those less introspective days, and there were certain conventions of hagiography which are inclined to come in the way of a lifelike portrait. But with Cuthbert we can still get some idea of a personality that left an abiding mark and inspired a devotion that remained active long after his death. To this day the name of this man who in his life was self-effacing even by the standard of the saints is widely commemorated. Kirkcudbright means the Church of Cuthbert and is our only county to owe its name to an individual. The noblest of all the great churches of Britain, Durham Cathedral, is dedicated to him, and contains his shrine, although it is a moot point whether his remains are still there or concealed in a secret hiding-place to which they were taken at the Reformation. The church below the castle rock in Edinburgh is another St Cuthbert's, and his name today is blazoned on the shopfronts and vans of a chain of co-operative stores in the Scottish capital.

It is curious that his early biographers should make no mention of Cuthbert's birthplace. It is considered that he was probably born in Ireland, although we first read of him in Scotland, herding sheep on the low hills of the Lammermuirs. Here one night he had a vision, a celestial company crossing the sky at an hour that proved to be that of the death of St Aidan in Lindisfarne.

Aidan, a monk of Iona, had been brought to Northumbria by King Oswald. In the year 617 Oswald as a young man had been driven from his kingdom and had taken refuge in Iona, where he became a Christian. On regaining his kingdom his first concern was its conversion, and he sent to Iona for a bishop. The first to come was unsuccessful and, returning to Iona to report, was rebuked by Aidan for being "more severe on your unlearned brothers than you ought to have been, in that you did not at first, conformably to the apostolic discipline, give them the milk of more gentle doctrine, till, being by degrees nourished with the word of God, they should be capable of greater perfection and able to practise God's sublimer precepts". Aidan himself was then sent to Northumbria. He did not go to York, where the see had already been established, but to the island of Lindisfarne, which for him held the attraction of another Iona, being both withdrawn and at the same time centrally placed for his sphere of action. Here, in the manner of Columba, he founded a monastery and made it the base for his work in evangelizing the waxing Kingdom of Northumbria.

His vision of Aidan's passage to heaven inspired Cuthbert with a sense of vocation. He went to Melrose and became an ordained monk in the monastery there, a foundation that had been made from Iona by Aidan himself, on a site a couple of miles from the Abbey of mediaeval times.

Ten years later Cuthbert was sent to Ripon in Yorkshire to found a new monastery. Now, however, the disagreement over the proper date for celebrating Easter was becoming acute, with St Augustine's mission in Canterbury observing the new reckoning promulgated by Rome in the year 567. The Celtic monks observed an earlier Roman reckoning. Although they were exhorted by Rome to accept the revised reckoning so that their usage might conform to that of the rest of the Church, they were never regarded in any sense as schismatic despite the long delay of many of their number in doing so. The Columban monks left Ripon when the new usage was imposed there. Cuthbert returned to Melrose and conducted a mission in the Lothians and beyond, living for a time in a hermitage at Dull in Perthshire, before becoming Prior of Melrose.

Under Oswald's successor, King Oswy, the Northumbrian

Kingdom reached its zenith, until its influence stretched by conquest and alliance from the Humber, far south in England, to
embrace Dalriada, Strathclyde, and the lands of the Southern
Picts, bringing their churches temporarily under the See of York.
The Easter issue came to a head when Oswy found himself
observing Lent while his queen, who came from the south and
the see of Canterbury, was celebrating Easter. In 664 he called
the Synod of Whitby to settle the dispute in his realm. Colman,
then Abbot of Lindisfarne, was chief spokesman for the Celtic
observance. He spoke with dignity and intelligence. The arguments of his principal opponent, Wilfrid, Bishop of York, were in
some details not particularly sound or wise. Had he been more
conciliatory much future friction might have been avoided. But,
with Colman conceding the primacy of Peter's chair, King Oswy
decided in favour of the Roman observance. St Colman returned
to Iona, and from thence to Ireland. Iona and the Northern Irish
Church continued to keep the Celtic calendar, although the
bishops of the Southern Irish Church had conformed as early as 634
after Pope Honorius had exhorted them "not to esteem their
small number, placed in the utmost borders of the earth, wiser
than all the ancient and modern Churches of Christ throughout
the world".

The Northern Irish conformed in 697, but Iona retained the
old reckoning for longer, which brought an end to its supremacy,
and from then on its influence dwindled. Cuthbert himself
accepted the decision reached at Whitby, and was later transferred
to Lindisfarne and "by the modest power of patience" brought
the more obtuse monks there to conformity. From Lindisfarne he
maintained a very active mission, making a deep impression by
the austerity of his life, a simplicity he observed even after he had
been appointed Bishop of Lindisfarne. He spent long periods of
solitary prayer in a hermitage on the small island of Farne. He
died there, in his hermitage, in the year 687.

To the present age, with its conception of achievement as the
fruit of our own activity, the idea of a man seeking the solitary
life of an anchorite sometimes seems odd or out of date. Yet we
should know in ourselves the frustration of distractions, and the

need for peace and withdrawal, often recommended even for our mental and physical health. For those with a sense of spiritual values, the necessity for isolation from the frenzy of mundane living should be still more apparent. St Benedict spent years alone in a cave before starting on one of the most decisive and widely influential careers in history. There were many hermits amongst the Celtic monks who, like Cuthbert, found their way to small islands where they might live in constant prayer. It is not for us to know the measure of their solitary achievement but it would be stupid to doubt it. Many islands have the remains of the little chapels of these Celtic hermits: their *teampuls* built beehive-fashion with false arches of overlapping flat stones forming vaulted roofs. The extremely isolated island of North Rona, lying alone between Orkneys and Hebrides, was the home supposedly of St Ronan himself in the eighth century, and his chapel was there, although replaced at a rather later date by the chapel that still stands. Even more barren, utterly forbidding, only approachable in the calmest weather, Sula Sgeir, home of gannets, a small sea-blasted rock without enough earth to hold water for a single spring, has its *teampul* carefully constructed by some forgotten hermit. In the Firth of Forth, within the old Northumbrian Kingdom, the Bass Rock was the bare home of the anchorite Baldred, who died in 756, and the small island of Inchcolm still has its cell, somewhat reconstructed. Inchcolm means Columba's Isle, and the hermit who gave shelter there to Alexander I at the beginning of the twelfth century was even then professedly a disciple of St Columba.

No doubt a cluster of myths gathered round his name in the years following Cuthbert's death, but many of the stories told in the early biographies are credible enough. His capacity for quiet gave him the confidence of birds and animals which, as Bede has it, we only lose through neglecting the service of the author of all creation. There is the story told of Cuthbert going to Coldingham on the Berwickshire coast to instruct the nuns there, whose abbess, Aebbe, was a sister of King Oswy. At night he would leave the neighbouring monastery in which he was staying, returning only with the morning. One of the monks, filled with curiosity, secretly followed him. He saw Cuthbert go down to the shore and wade deep into the sea, there singing God's praise to the sound of the waves. After a long time Cuthbert came back to the beach and knelt in prayer. Out of the sea came two otters who rubbed themselves against the saint's feet as though to dry and warm them. The sight filled the doubting monk with shame, and he came out of hiding and begged Cuthbert's forgiveness, which was granted on condition that he told no man what he had seen so long as Cuthbert lived. Years later on the island of Farne Cuthbert built a little guest house for the monks who came to visit him. A pair of ravens persisted in taking the straw from its roof to build their nest, until at last the saint, by word of mouth, banished them from his island. Three days later the ravens returned, humbly croaking as if begging pardon, and were reconciled, never again being so unneighbourly as to steal from their friend.

More miraculous stories are the more likely to get glosses and romantic façades attached to them, much in the way that facts now become ornamented in print as well as in speech. Yet the disciples of Cuthbert at least did not pursue the constricted lives of many of us today who live blinded even to the miracle of life about us, and for the sake of our very complacency must deny the possibility of the miraculous so that, while not admitting God's laws, we fervently deny his right to infringe them. To the converts of Northumbria the miracles of faith and redemption, of the Body and Blood, were fresh in mind, and their acceptance dissolved primitive superstition for them just as their acceptance can still dissolve the sophisticated, but yet basically primitive, fear of the unknown and the mysterious in the form in which it constitutes the superstition of our time. For superstition, that which *stands over*, the sense of an arbitrary power dominating our lives, is not confined to matters of magic. Druids using faculties that have largely atrophied in civilized man might as reasonably strike fear into the ancient Celts as scientists, using those alternative faculties that have been inordinately developed in their stead, strike fear into the civilized world. Yet to the eye of faith these fears reach levels that are equally irrational, because faithless and therefore unable to accept life and death as unity.

Amongst the relatively unspoilt and simple people of the Northumbrian Kingdom Cuthbert made an impression that far outlived that kingdom itself. It is a mystery that it is only in his practice of virtue that man's true personality develops, when it might have seemed that the closer he identified himself with God the less his finite distinction would show. But it is the evil man who loses identity, who is submerged and depersonalized by those world-forces that Tolstoy liked to argue were history's real motivation. He may, like Adolf Hitler, set himself at the head of movements, but he is still their victim, carried on by forces he at last can only lead and cannot control or deflect. The more he struts, the more orders he gives and the more he identifies himself with his position, the more of the world's prisoner he becomes. Men like Cuthbert are the true leaven that works upon the lump of man in his self-interest: without such as he we should never have known our civilization; even much watered-down, it is still his creed exalting higher motives that makes its values possible. Cuthbert himself was not primarily concerned with the mission of civilizing: it was a by-product of a higher aim, the service of God that often took him alone to island or wilderness, and that made him a willing prisoner of the Word, but not of the world.

CHAPTER III

OUTPOSTS

COLLOQUIALLY St Magnus might be called the Saint of Bad Form, for it was by flouting accepted convention that he established his title to martyrdom. The convention in question was comprehensive and formidable, that of the fighting men of the Norse lands. It was the source of their power and had made their name feared all along the coasts of northern Europe. It was their religious creed as well as their social code: its apotheosis the warrior's reward, when the winged Valkyries bore his soul to the eternal junketings of Valhalla.

It was a soldier's creed, and a stoic's. It was expressed and exhorted in the sagas, those chronicles recited by the skalds praising the deeds of the viking heroes. They contained such details as the remark of the dying warrior looking down at the spear being driven through his breast and saying: "Long-leaved spears seem to be coming into fashion": or the reply made to a sympathizer moved at the sight of a hideous stomach-wound to ask: "Does it hurt?" and being told: "Only when I laugh". It saluted such courage and an often bloodthirsty code of honour, but it had no place whatever for mercy, forgiveness or clemency. For all its bravery this sustaining heroism of man dwindles before the lonely figure on the cross and the death that was only an affront to a people.

Before Magnus was born, about 1076, Christianity had made some inroads upon the old order, and Norway for a time was ruled by a saint, King Olav. But old habits prevail and Christian missions were commonly carried out in a pagan spirit. Prospective converts were offered the choice of baptism or death, so that both their enthusiasm and their doctrine were liable to be scant; certain essentials had been left out.

It was Magnus Erlendson who swept aside the established order by an action quite unparalleled elsewhere in the sagas: one, indeed, that was hardly to be encouraged in martial lays. The young Norwegian king, another Magnus, nicknamed Barelegs because he had adopted the Celtic kilt, had sailed from Norway to establish again his overlordship of the Scottish islands. Stopping in Orkney he had sent Magnus's father, Erlend, and his uncle, Paul, back to Norway in some disgrace for their indifference in safeguarding Norwegian interests in the Western Islands. Taking Magnus in his own longship as his personal attendant, the king then sailed west, landing on one island after another and doing great slaughter. This was in 1098 and one concession was made to Christian sentiment in that Iona was spared from plunder and bloodshed, although with the rest of the islands it became once again Norwegian property. The mainland coast of Kintyre was also ravaged, and the Isle of Man subdued. Then to crown a highly successful raid, the Norwegian fleet sailed to Wales. Here, off the coast of Anglesey, it was attacked by a fleet under Welsh and English leadership. This was the first serious conflict demanded of the expedition, and all hands were called to the fight. It was then that Magnus the Orcadian sat down, unarmed, on the deck, and when the king asked him what he was doing, replied that he would not fight as he had no quarrel with any man present.

It was conduct that might have brought summary execution, but the king contented himself with contemptuously ordering Magnus to go and hide if he did not dare to fight. This also Magnus, in order to make clear the reason for his action, refused to do, saying he would stay where he was. "Let God shield me; I shall not die if he wills that I should live." He took up a psalter and sang while the battle raged. He made no attempt to shield himself, but came through unscathed.

The battle off Anglesey was a victory for the vikings, although a costly one, and gave them possession of the fertile island. The fleet sailed north again, with Magnus in deep disgrace. Christian of a kind though he was, the king could not accept that his faith should drive Magnus to such humiliating conduct. Their relationship must have been extremely strained, and Magnus was

probably virtually under arrest. One morning as the fleet lay off
the Scottish coast, it was found that Magnus had disappeared.
A search was made with the help of slot-hounds. Magnus in
making his escape had hurt his foot and taken refuge in a tree.
One of the hounds tracked him and bayed beneath the tree.
Magnus threw a stick, and the hound ran off with its tail between
its legs. The fleet sailed on, and Magnus made his way to Edinburgh, to the Court of King Edgar, the first of the three sons of St
Margaret to ascend the Scottish throne.

Magnus was himself of partly Scottish blood, and related
to the king. Edgar, who was known as the Peaceable, had refused
to make a war, which would probably have been futile, with the
Norwegian king over his latest depredations, and freely ceded
the Hebrides to him. Edgar had inherited the religious and
cultured interests of his mother and gladly gave hospitality to
Magnus, who must have found Edinburgh congenial, with the
churchmen and scholars who were welcome visitors to the
Court. He also travelled to England and Wales, making friend-
ships there.

When in the ninth century the Norwegians had first annexed
the Orkneys and Shetlands, they supplanted and probably
largely absorbed the original Pictish stock. These seem to have
been a gentle if primitive people. Excavations of homesteads
buried in the sand have given us some idea of how they lived.
Excavations of viking longhouses alongside the Pictish dwellings
suggest, oddly enough, that the more developed vikings were far
less cleanly and house-proud: plainly they were more interested
in their ships than in their homes. Orkney was made a Norwegian
earldom, which included Shetland and, for a time, Caithness,
although this mainland unit of the earldom was latterly held in
fief to the King of Scots. Magnus's father and uncle had been
joint earls and had ruled in remarkable accord, giving a welcome
period of peace to a people who were beginning to grow weary
of swashbuckling; although Magnus as a youth had been sent on
marauding expeditions as an essential part of his education. The
accord between the two earls had been broken by the conduct of
the cousin of Magnus, Haakon. Haakon resented the prospect of

The Mirror Symbol on a Pictish Stone at Aboyne, Aberdeenshire

Photo: Malcolm Murray

Pictish Cross at Dunfallandy, Perthshire

Photo: Malcolm Murray

having to share the earldom. At a meeting of the Orcadian parliament, or Thing, Haakon, before the Norwegian expedition of 1098, had been politely requested to take a holiday, and had spent a few years in Norway and Sweden.

The sagas relate that while in Sweden Haakon learnt of the presence in a forest there of a spaeman, one who practised the old pagan rites and had a reputation for being able to foretell future events. Like Macbeth, Haakon visited a soothsayer to discover his dynastic future.

"Why not learn your fate from St Olav?" the spaeman challenged. "Or is he not so powerful as you like to think?" However lukewarm his faith, Haakon would allow no slur on St Olav who was his own great-great-grandfather, and he replied with some grace that if St Olav would not forecast his future to him it was not for lack of the saint's power to do so but on account of his own unworthiness. Eventually, after passing into a trance, the spaeman foretold that Haakon would become sole chief of the Orkneys, but not soon; that his descendants would succeed him; that from his return home great things would come to pass, but that he would "let that wickedness be done" for which he would have to choose whether or not he would atone to the God in whom he believed.

Haakon accepted what he liked of the prophecy, but averred that he thought things would go better with him than was suggested. He went back to Norway and encouraged King Magnus Barelegs to make the Scottish expedition, hoping thereby to gain the king's gratitude and the Orkney earldom for himself alone. Instead, the king reasserted his own overlordship, in 1099 making his second son king over his Scottish dominions, although entrusting the eight-year-old boy to the care of Haakon and of Magnus's older brother, Erlend. Four years later, at the age of thirty, King Magnus Barelegs was killed while invading Ireland. Erlend was killed at the same time. The king's son returned to Norway, and Haakon was left with more or less absolute power in the Northern Isles, killing the king's steward so as to bring the share of his cousin Magnus into his own hands, and governing with greed and harshness.

C

Reluctant though he perhaps was to do so, news of events in Orkney eventually brought Magnus north to claim his heritage. He came to Caithness and lingered there "that it should not be shown that he sought his inheritance after warrior's wise, but as a friend and dear lover of law and justice". When at length he proceeded to Orkney, Haakon prepared to fight. But the leading men of the islands, to whom Magnus was much the more acceptable ruler, called a parley, and it was agreed that Magnus should go to refer the matter to the three boy kings who now jointly ruled Norway. This he did, and was confirmed in his earldom in 1108, returning to Orkney to take up his duties as joint-earl with Haakon.

Magnus had married during his exile in Scotland. His wife's name was Ingarth, and they married with mutual vows of chastity under which their marriage was never consummated. It was for this that he was sometimes known as Magnus the Maiden. Again, it was an unconventional act, but one that exalted the highest aspect of human love. Ingarth seems to have died some time before her husband.

For a while the two earls ruled in concord. Together they chased and killed two marauding vikings who harried their people. But Haakon's jealousy persisted. Magnus went at one time to London and spent about a year at the Court of Henry I, whose wife, as sister of the Scots king, was a cousin of his. He made a very favourable impression at the English Court, and this was perhaps the reason for the dedication, not long after his death, of the church of St Magnus Martyr in London. But again bad news reached him of Haakon's tyranny in the Orkneys, and he returned. Haakon was reluctantly compelled to renew his bond of peace.

At this time growing acceptance of Christian ethics had made the word viking, formerly a term of honour, become increasingly synonymous with evil-doer. Magnus tried to stop viking raids being made from the Orkneys. Haakon had few such scruples, and his hatred for Magnus was played upon by the viking elements in the islands. The situation between the two earls growing worse again, a Thing was called during Lent in the year 1115.

These Norse parliaments devised to settle disputes amicably quite often ended in bloodshed, and the men who attended them came armed. Haakon once again made peace, appreciating that his supporters were heavily outnumbered. Immediately afterwards he sent word calling upon Magnus to meet him during Easter week on the island of Egilsay, to confirm their agreement. Each was to bring only two ships, with their crews, and each was bound by the most solemn oaths to come in peace.

Unlike the wilder Shetlands, which in a manner more resembling the Outer Hebrides stretch north and south in a rough-linked chain, the Orkneys form a compact group, low-lying and comparatively fertile. Sheltered bays lie back from the inter-island tide races. Kirkwall, capital of the Isles since Norwegian days, having then a tidal basin for the wintering of longboats, sits central to its little domain on the principal island. Egilsay is one of several lesser isles that lie between the Orkney mainland and the major islands scattered to the north. It is a long, thin, grassy island, with flagstone beaches, and owes its name to the church built there in early times.

Magnus arrived first at Egilsay for the meeting with Haakon. As he waited on the new green grass he saw not two but ten fully-manned longships coming up the sound. Then he knew that Haakon came for his blood. His men wanted to fight it out, but he refused to let them face such impossible odds and commanded them to leave him. He himself went into the church to pray. The roofless church that stands today with its singular, dramatic round tower, is probably an early rebuilding of that in which Magnus actually spent his last night. In the morning he heard Mass before going out to meet Haakon and his men.

Even by pagan Norse standards Haakon's treachery was abject since it involved the breaking of oaths regarded as irrevocable and utterly binding. Magnus, the Christian, pled that Haakon rather than damn his own soul by an act of murder should allow him to go away alone, and he would make the pilgrimage to Rome and the Holy Land to pray for the souls of them both, and never return to Orkney. Haakon refused. Magnus suggested then that he should send him prisoner into Scotland, under close

guard. Haakon again refused. Then Magnus offered to have his
eyes plucked out, or to be maimed, before being sent to prison.
Haakon was prepared to agree, but some of his viking companions
insisted upon death. Haakon then ordered his banner-bearer to
kill Magnus, but Ofeig, the banner-bearer, angrily refused. So
Haakon's cook, Lifolf, was ordered to be the executioner. He
burst into tears, but was ill-placed to refuse. Magnus comforted
him, then asked permission to pray, and lay down full-length on
the grass, praying "not only for himself and his friends but rather
there and then for his foes and banemen, and forgave them with
all his heart for what they had misdone towards him". Lastly he
asked God's forgiveness and mercy for himself, then he rose and
called upon Lifolf, "Stand thou before me, and hew me on the
head a great wound, for it becomes not to chop off chiefs' heads
like thieves'; strengthen thyself, wretched man. I have prayed to
God to have mercy on thee." He made the sign of the cross, and
Lifolf struck the axe-blow whose gash still shows on the skull
preserved in the mediaeval Cathedral of Kirkwall. Haakon at
once ordered his cousin's body to be buried where it lay, and not
in consecrated ground.

Thora, the mother of Magnus, had invited her son and nephew
to a banquet to celebrate the lasting peace that seemed about to be
joined. Haakon with his men came to the banquet. Thora silently
waited upon her son's murderer. Only at the close of the banquet
did she speak, to ask him to allow Magnus's body to be buried in
church ground. He burst into tears, and gave her his permission.

None the less, for a time Haakon was vindictive to the friends
and supporters of his dead rival. But a change came over him. At
last he made public penance, travelling to Rome for Papal
absolution, and going on as pilgrim to the Holy Land. He returned
to Orkney and for the few years left to him ruled with justice
and clemency.

After Haakon's death, the nephew of Magnus, Earl Ronald,
came back to Orkney from Norway and ordered the building,
under the supervision of his father, Kol, of the lovely little
romanesque Cathedral of St Magnus that is still the shrine of the
relics of two saints, Magnus and Ronald himself. As a cathedral

city Kirkwall entered upon its greatest days. The Orkneys were not then, as they are now, on the periphery of Europe, but centrally situated upon important trade routes between Scandinavia and western lands. Indeed, Kirkwall almost anticipated Spain in the re-discovery of America. Centuries earlier, viking longships had penetrated to the far northern coasts of the American continent, and, fifty years before Columbus sailed, the Earl of Orkney commissioned the Venetian navigator Zenoni to explore the western seas in search of the lost continent. Orkneys and Shetlands only came under the Scottish Crown in 1468. Even then Kirkwall retained a thriving life. One of the last of its bishops, Bishop Reid, was about to found a university there, and it was his endowment that founded the University of Edinburgh instead.

By his life and death it was Magnus's achievement to express to his people the absoluteness of the Christian claim and demand. No doubt that may be said to be the example of all the saints. But with Magnus the process is clear and simple. The Norsemen of the Scottish islands had accepted, as so many of us do, something of the general ethic of Christianity. After some initial compulsory conversion, they had conceded the superiority of their new faith over their earlier pagan beliefs, and come to hold it willingly if not fervently. It was Magnus who revealed in his person the truth that the disciple of Christ may have to repudiate both those things that, by the standards of the society in which he lives, may seem to be his duties, and those that he might regard as his rights. This is the demand of a supernatural faith, not a mere ethical code, pragmatic, convenient, or utilitarian, but something not limited by human usage and acquired convention. It was the common recognition of the supernatural in the Blessed Sacrament that the priest lifts above the altar that made in that time of which Magnus saw the beginning, and which prevailed for some two centuries, such remarkable unity throughout central and western Europe. Changes had to come; no orderly progress, but mutations and growing-pains, erratic, often bitter and confusing, as inevitable to the growing-up of the world as they are to the growing-up of the individual. These changes extend man's apprehension in many ways, but they afford no vision loftier than that seen by Magnus and the Celtic saints before him: the child's vision that Christ demanded of each man that he should at last regain for his own.

CHAPTER IV

UNITY

IN time Queen Margaret comes before Earl Magnus but in history her place is with a later phase. St Magnus represents the establishment of Christianity in the remoter and wilder parts, his achievement continues the mission of the Celtic saints; he, within the Norse framework, extends their work in the earlier Celtic environment. St Margaret stands at the beginning of a new era, a united Scotland with its central government on the shores of the Firth of Forth. The year 1066 that saw the Norman Conquest and the birth-pangs of mediaeval England contributed almost accidentally to the more peaceful genesis of mediaeval Scotland: for it was to escape from the Norman invader that Margaret with her mother and brother and sister took refuge at the Scottish Court.

Margaret's father was a Saxon prince who while in exile on the Continent married a German princess. Their children were first brought up in the Court of St Stephen, King of Hungary, and came to England some ten years before the Norman Invasion, where their education was completed at the Court of Edward the Confessor. Margaret was about twenty-two when she came to Scotland, whose king, a widower, fell in love with her and eventually, for she had wished to become a nun, persuaded her to marry him.

It was a singularly blessed union. Margaret brought with her the freshets of European civilization; she was highly intelligent, well-read, and exceptionally qualified for her job as queen having had before her the example of two kings who were also saints. In her husband she had one of the greatest of the Scottish kings, Malcolm Canmore, "the great leader", forceful and competent in bringing order to his country, who, through the power

39

of his love for his queen, came to share her exalted ideals.

We know many details of Margaret's life because her confessor, Turgot, subsequently Bishop of St Andrews, wrote her biography at the request of her elder daughter, Matilda, Queen of Henry I of England. His account is somewhat formal and courtly, its author very conscious for whom he is writing, but it gives us a delightful picture of an active and holy royal family life. The queen's chamber became "a workshop of sacred art: in which copes for the cantors, chasubles, stoles, altar-cloths, together with other priestly vestments and church-ornaments of an admirable beauty, were always to be seen, either already made or in course of preparation".

The queen devoted part of every day to the poor, the diseased and the crippled:

"She ordered that nine little orphans utterly destitute should be brought to her at the first hour of the day, and that some soft food such as children at that tender age like, should daily be prepared for them. When the little ones were carried to her she did not think it beneath her to take them upon her knee, and to get their pap ready for them, and this she put into their mouths with the spoon which she herself used."

In the Bodleian Library there is a manuscript of the Gospels which was purchased in 1887 and then supposed to be of four-teenth-century date. It was later identified as belonging to the eleventh century and by some Latin verses written on a fly-leaf as being the very book mentioned by Turgot as having fallen into a river and being recovered some little time later remarkably undamaged save for a slight crinkling of the first and last pages. It had lost the fine bejewelled case with which Malcolm Canmore liked to honour the books that delighted his wife:

Although he could not read, he would turn over and examine books that the queen used either for her devotions or her study; and whenever he heard her express especial liking for a particular book, he also would look at it with special interest, kissing it, and often taking it into his hands. . . .

By the help of God she made him most attentive to the works of mercy, justice, almsgiving, and other virtues. From her he learnt how to keep the vigils of the night in constant prayer.

In church no one was so silent and composed as she, no one so wrapt in prayer. Whilst she was in the house of God she would never speak of worldly matters, or do anything which savoured of the earth; she was there simply to pray, and in praying to pour forth her tears.

Thanks to their mother's care, her children surpassed in good behaviour many who were their elders; they were always affectionate and peaceable among themselves, and everywhere the younger paid due respect to the elder.

But Queen Margaret's piety was not confined to alms and her family. Scotland was faced with ecclesiastical problems that required tact and resolution for their settling. The history of the Scottish Church between the eighth and the eleventh centuries lacks such detailed documentation as we have for at least part of the period of the Celtic monks. It saw the development of a secular clergy, first introduced by Wilfrid of York after the Synod of Whitby, and of episcopal sees of administration developed to meet the needs of a growing society. It saw also the coming of the Culdees. A popular fallacy has derived the Culdees from the Celtic monks, and even identified the two. But the Culdees were not exclusively Scottish or Irish but were found also on the Continent, where they were known as *Deicolae*, "God-worshippers", anchorites who made a special practice of solitary prayer (*Culdee* is a simple inversion of *Deicolae*). They very often took over monastic settlements which had been vacated by Celtic communities, and for long they represented the monastic element in the Scottish Church, only being replaced when Queen Margaret and her sons introduced the established orders, Benedictines, Augustinians, Cistercians, who thus came comparatively late to Scotland. The Culdees cannot properly be considered as part of the Celtic phase of the Church's development but were the monastic concomitant to the next phase, the organization of a secular priesthood.

Lacking the golden guidance of the Rule of St Benedict, the Culdees were the more liable to fall into excesses and vagaries. On the Continent various steps were taken to bring the *Deicolae* under firm discipline, but they were soon superseded by the growth of the great monastic orders. In Scotland, while many of them were admirable and holy men, they tended to become somewhat ingrown, and by Queen Margaret's time a new difference over the keeping of Lent had arisen. This time it was nothing to do with the correct reckoning of the phases of the moon, but with the day on which Lent was to start, a problem that had arisen in earlier times in different places. Turgot gives us an account of a council called by Margaret.

The queen introduced the subject under discussion by premising that all who serve one God in one faith along with the Catholic Church ought not to vary from that Church by new or far-fetched usages. She then laid it down, in the first place, that the fast of Lent was not kept as it ought to be by those who were in the habit of beginning it on the Monday of the first week in Lent; thus differing from the Holy Catholic Church, which begins it on the fourth day of the previous week at the commencement of Lent. The opponents objected thus: "The fast which we observe we keep according to the authority of the Gospel, which reports that Christ fasted for six weeks". She replied by saying: "Herein you differ widely from the Gospel, wherein we read that Our Lord fasted for forty days, a thing which notoriously you do not do. For seeing that during the six weeks you deduct the six Sundays from the fast, it is clear that thirty-six days only remain on which to fast. Plainly, then, the fast which you keep is not that fast of forty days which is commanded by the Gospel, but consists of six and thirty days only. It comes then to this, you ought to do as we do. Like us, you should begin your fast four days before the first Sunday of Lent; that is, if you wish, according to Our Lord's example, to observe an abstinence of forty days. If you refuse to do this, you will be the only persons who are acting in opposition to the authority of Our Lord Himself and the tradition of the entire Holy Church." Convinced by this plain demonstration of the truth, these persons began henceforth the solemnities of the fast as Holy Church observes them everywhere.

The Queen then dealt with a more fundamental and dangerous

point of divergence, an attitude ever recurrent in the Manichean heresies that arise within the Church.

She asked them to explain why it was that on the Festival of Easter they neglected to receive the Sacrament of the Body and Blood of Christ according to the usage of the Holy and Apostolic Church? They answered her thus: "The Apostle when speaking of persons who eat and drink unworthily, says that they eat and drink judgment to themselves. Now, since we admit that we are sinners, we fear to approach that mystery, lest we should eat and drink judgment to ourselves." "What!" said the queen to them: "Shall no one that is a sinner taste that holy mystery? If so, then it follows that no one at all should receive it, for no one is pure from sin; no, not even the infant, who has lived but one day upon the earth. And if no one ought to receive it, why did the Lord make this proclamation in the Gospel?—Except you shall eat the flesh of the Son of Man and drink His Blood, you shall not have life in you. But if you would understand the passage which you have quoted from the Apostle according to the interpretation of the Fathers, then you must give it quite a different meaning. The Evangelist does not hold that all sinners are unworthy of the sacraments of salvation; for after saying 'He that eateth and drinketh judgment to himself', he adds, 'Not discerning the Body of the Lord'; that is, not distinguishing it by faith from bodily food. It is the man who, without confession and penance, and carrying with him the defilements of his sins presumes to approach the sacred mysteries, such a one, I say it is, who eats and drinks judgment to himself. Whereas we who many days previously have made confession of our sins and have been cleansed from their stains by chastening penance, by trying fasts, by almsgiving and tears —approaching in the Catholic faith to the Lord's Table on the day of His Resurrection, receive the Body and Blood of Jesus Christ, the immaculate Lamb, not to judgment but to the remission of our sins, and as a health-giving preparation for eternal happiness." To these arguments they could not answer a word, and knowing now the meaning of the Church's practices observed them ever after in the sacrament of salvation.

The tremendous importance of Margaret to Scotland lay in

her opening of the door on to the wider world of Europe, opening it not by the battering ram of war and conquest, but with the peace of sanctity, so that these new influences were vastly more acceptable than ever they could have been washed in with blood. The isolation brought about by conflict and division had cut off and impoverished the life of the Scottish Church and the, as yet embryo, nation. The enthusiasm of the Celtic saints was little more than a memory which although it was cherished held them as almost legendary figures, heroes of a distant past rather than as exponents of a present way of life. Margaret's practical application of their occluded lesson admittedly displaced some of the Celtic saints from the Scottish Calendar, to which they were returned as symbols of nationhood during the Wars of Independence. Yet it is only ignorance that can see Margaret's mission as deleterious to the integrity of the Scottish nation. Rather, she enlivened Scotland with civilization and brought a much-needed prestige to her Throne. Nations do not flourish in isolation which is the achievement not of a healthy body politic but of violence and oppression. The proof of Margaret's gift was to be seen in the two hundred succeeding years, those happiest centuries of Scotland's history.

Yet Margaret herself was to die, as other saints have died, when it seemed that all her achievement was to be effaced, so that her last prayer was a cry of anguish and resignation. Her husband and eldest son had been killed in battle, and a rebel army marched on Edinburgh as she lay dying in the Castle. She commended her soul to God: "Praise and blessing be to thee, O Almighty God, that thou hast been pleased to make me endure so bitter anguish at the hour of my departure, thereby, as I trust, to purify me in some measure from the corruption of my sins; and thou, Lord Jesus Christ, who through the will of thy Father, hast given life to the world by thy death, O! deliver me."

But the mother's care was not wasted. Three of the sons whose education had been so important to Margaret became king in turn, two entered religion, one daughter became Queen of England and the other a nun. Margaret herself had introduced the first monks of the great Continental orders to Scotland when

she brought Benedictines to the then capital city of Dunfermline.
Her sons founded many more monasteries, particularly the third
of them to rule, David I. No king of his day made so many
religious foundations. The monks were the prime means of
civilizing, but the development of towns and trade and of feudal
order were also his achievement. Under him Edinburgh first
became the established capital of Scotland, but he retained and
enhanced the Royal Palace of Dunfermline and raised its priory
into an abbey. In later years palace and church and abbey constituted together a singularly noble range of Gothic building.
Today it is only the romanesque nave, built in David's reign,
that remains intact, the pillared aisle still with a calm splendour
of devotion.

It was to Dunfermline that Margaret's body was taken to
safety from the insurgents under cover of mist. A new tomb was
erected in the Lady Aisle after she was formally canonized in the
year 1250. It was smashed and desecrated at the Reformation.
Mary Queen of Scots succeeded in rescuing Margaret's head, still
remarkably preserved, with fair hair. A Benedictine monk took
care of it on Mary's flight to England and passed it on to the
Jesuit missionaries, one of whom brought it to Antwerp. Early
in the seventeenth century it was taken to the Scots College at
Douay. It disappeared in the French Revolution. Other remains
of Margaret and her husband went to Spain, from whence in the
last century a relic was brought back to Scotland by Bishop Gillis.

On the very summit of the Castle rock in Edinburgh, the city's
oldest building, the little chapel that Margaret had built for her
own use has survived sackings and razings and reforms, and even
a period of duty as a gunner's store, and, like a keystone to the
city whose history owes so much to St Margaret, hangs over the
noise and stour of the contemporary scene.

Every year on a Sunday early in June, thousands of people
come from all parts of southern Scotland to Dunfermline. Largely
they come from smoke-blackened straggling conurbations, parts
of Scotland that have grown old and ugly with unreckoning
industrialism. Not for the most part deeply versed in history,
they still do honour to the memory of a mediaeval queen. They

see her perhaps through the eyes of sentimentally-inclined illustrators as a willowy golden-haired girl wearing a crown and ministering to the poor. But they know that she embodied in her life the charity that does not change but is quite simply the same in mediaeval palace or twentieth-century housing-scheme, and know themselves her true heirs in the sacrament celebrated not in the mediaeval shrine built for her body's repose, and from which it also was thrown out in days of strange and witless frenzy, but in the smoky sunlight of the local football field.

CHAPTER V

PRAYER

THERE is a bell shrine, a bronze casket fashioned for the keeping of a cherished and more ancient Celtic bell, that is now in the Museum of Antiquities in Edinburgh. The Celtic patterning is scant, and the figure, of Christ crucified, is like those that decorate the great romanesque bronze doors of almost the same date, some of which are still to be seen widely dispersed over Europe. It has the same abruptness, a simple urgency and certitude as though it had been formed not by the deliberate hands of the artist but rather by the reposeful hands of a monk at prayer; without afterthought or revision. The cross itself is in very low relief, ghostly; the only other feature is the hand of God, two fingers outstretched, over the head of the crucified; a gesture of both compassion and rebuke.

The Kilmichael–Glassary bell shrine is art of an extraordinary economy of statement, like all these romanesque bronzes: it is art contemplative not meditative, not discursing but containing its story; in this doing what is much attempted if rarely achieved by artists of the present day. These bronzes were the work of artists who were also monks, and who worked at the time of Europe's greatest unity. It was the time at which Scotland came closest to the rest of European culture.

Although mediaeval monasticism came comparatively late to Scotland, it came at a time of great vitality and proliferation, and under King David I remarkable numbers of foundations were made. David was allegedly criticized for his endowments by a later King, James I, but as the historian of *Scotland in the Middle Ages*, Cosmo Innes, observes:

> Even if King David had given more of his property, I do not know that he would have deserved the character which

47

his successor is said to have given him of being "ane sair sanct for the crown". However it may have become the fashion in later times to censure or ridicule this sudden and magnificent endowment of a Church, the poor natives of Scotland of the twelfth century had no cause to regret it. . . . At such a time it was undoubtedly one great step in improvement to throw a vast mass of property into the hands of that class whose duty and interest alike inculcated peace, and who had the influence and the power to command. Repose was the one thing most wanted, and the people found it under the protection of the crozier. . . . If a sovereign is to look for something more than mere revenue from royal lands, it may be doubted if they could be turned at that time more to the benefit of the country than in the administration of the religious houses.

David's raising of Dunfermline to an abbey made the Benedictines there "to the Scottish monarchy something of what Westminster and St Denis were in England and France", to quote Professor Knowles. The Cistercians were a particular favourite of King David, who had close associations with Aelred of Rievaulx, from whence monks came to found the great Abbey of Melrose under a notable abbot, St Waldef, the king's own stepson. Newbattle and Dundrennan were others of the group of eleven Cistercian houses in Scotland. Augustinian Canons were brought from England to Holyrood, and from France to Cambuskenneth and Jedburgh. Kelso was the first of a number of houses of the Order of Tiron, also founded from France, which later included the important Abbey of Arbroath. David brought the first nuns to Scotland, Cistercians whose mother house he established at Berwick. After his time came the foundations of the Valliscaulians (notably at Pluscarden), and of the various friars: Dominicans, Franciscans, Carmelites and Augustinians.

Although in some respects Scotland was too late to benefit to the full from the intellectual and artistic stimulus of the monks, particularly from the great age of the Benedictines, she was in time to make some return for the benefits she had received, when monks and friars went from Scotland to the Continent. Notable amongst these were two men of a greater universality of mind than even the keenest of our thinkers, David Hume and Thomas

St Magnus's Cathedral, Kirkwall
Looking N.E. from the South Transept

Photo: Edwin Smith

Dunfermline Abbey

Norman Pillars in the Nave, looking from S.W. to N.E.

Photo: Edwin Smith

Carlyle, of later times: Richard of St Victor and Duns Scotus, the *doctor subtilis*. Richard of St Victor was hailed by Dante as "more than human in his powers of speculation", and he has a permanent place in the development of Christian mysticism as the first writer to have made an effort to systematize mystical prayer, an achievement perhaps not uncharacteristic of a Lowland Scot.

The prayer of the contemplative is recognized in all the higher religions as man's most direct approach to God. Yet, of its hidden nature, mysticism is most prone to excess, distortion, and even, if all system and safeguards be jettisoned, to diabolism. Always a *via media* must be found between the formal, ethical, moralist's approach to God, and the illuminism that denies to reason and experience their proper place; for our faith lies in neither ethical code nor ivory tower but in the redemption of the whole man, body and soul, by Christ who is at once the Supreme Spirit and flesh of our flesh.

Although there are often long periods of apparent stagnation, there is perceptible a growth in mankind's mystical experience in the sense in which it is communicable, even although, since its only object is the individual's union with God, the heights of that experience can never change. But man's knowledge and understanding of it may increase, and with them its powers of penetration through all his realms of thought: its relevance to his life become clearer as he sees his own limits more sharply defined against the illimitable knowledge of God.

The twelfth century saw the beginnings of a speculative spirituality that sprang from the monks known as the Victorines. The Abbey of St Victor had come into being through the resolve of William of Champeaux of the Paris schools to leave the world of wordy academic conflict for a more reflective life. This was in the year 1108. William's particular antagonist had been his own pupil, Peter Abelard, a scholar today best remembered for his tragic love affair with Heloïse. Brilliantly gifted as he was, the false note that sounds in Abelard's letters to Heloïse reveals that pride of intellect that easily deludes man in his pursuit of perfection, absorbing him in the idea of God, with all its intellectual niceties, until it excludes a sense of the person of God. This

D

sacrifice of substance for shadow is a particular danger to clever men, and it was in order to renew his intimacy with God in prayer that William of Champeaux withdrew to a hermitage at the foot of Mont Ste Geneviève outside the old bounds of Paris. He had no intention of founding a community, but was pressed to do so, and was so besieged by postulants that after five years his hermitage became an abbey. He himself was almost immediately called to be Bishop of Châlons, but offset an active episcopacy by making retreats to St Bernard's abbey of Clairvaux.

The monks of St Victor were Canons Regular, Augustinians, but they were influenced towards a more contemplative life both by their origin and by contact with the Cistercians of Clairvaux. William's successor in the abbacy, Gilduin, became a favourite with the French king, Louis VI, and was employed by him in the reform of the secular clergy. The abbey grew rich and powerful but under Gilduin this was not allowed to lead to abuse, and its canons were held in high esteem and constantly "borrowed" to help where reform and good example were needed, besides being employed in the founding of some forty-four dependent houses. Outstanding amongst them all was Hugh of St Victor, who revived and amplified the teaching of "Denis the Areopagite", the Biblical name taken by a Syrian monk of the fourth or fifth century.

It was on Hugh's work that Richard based his own writings, although Hugh's death in 1141 probably occurred before Richard came to the monastery from Scotland as a very young man. Hugh had said that love "surpasses knowledge, and is greater than understanding. We love more than we understand, and love draws near and enters where knowledge remains outside." But the Victorines never went to the length of depreciating knowledge and experience or approached the quietist position in their appraisal of contemplative prayer. Hugh was a scholar himself who declared that all sciences are part of theology, meaning that all knowledge contributes to our knowledge of God. Richard's acute psychological insight contributes to his ability to distinguish man's own part in his prayer from the part that is God's. It is a distinction admirably summarized in the following passage (given in the translation of Miss Clare Kirchberger[1]), in which he contrasts the part taken by meditation with that of contemplation.

Nor do we deny that there are some things concerning the nature of the future life—indeed there are many and great things which we can both seek to investigate and find by reasoning and analyse by discussion. For the invisible things of God are known and understood by the things that are made. Therefore we must never neglect those things that may be found by investigation, just as we must not intrude by our own power upon those things which transcend our intelligence and human reasoning. The former are known by reason, the latter are above reason. We must diligently enquire into the former by close examination, but for the latter, we must wait for the divine shewing with humility. The former belong to meditation, the latter to contemplation. The soul will never be fully enflamed with desire for the eternal riches, unless it has given thoughtful consideration to their nature and number. And just as it will never deserve to be raised to contemplate them without great desire, so truly it will not be perfectly enflamed with desire of eternal things without strenuous effort. . . .

First we must seek and find out by trial the method of making our meditation, and afterwards we must turn it to contemplation so that we may be able to practise it quickly and at will. . . . Contemplation has one purpose, meditation another. The work of meditation is to seek out hidden things, that of contemplation to wonder at clear truths. So then meditation is the careful investigation of hidden truth and contemplation the joyful wondering at transparent truth. But hidden things do become manifest, either through our meditation or by divine shewing. Therefore where we have the presence of the grace of revelation we do not need the service of meditation. But where divine revelation is lacking, the human mind, quite naturally, turns to the services of investigation. But whatever the human mind may come to know of moral teaching by the investigation of meditation, these fruits must be dwelt upon in contemplation and the soul strengthened in the certainty of those things and in its desire. . . . A man arrives in meditation at the knowledge of what he ought use-

[1]Faber and Faber, 1957.

fully to do. But the effect of contemplation is to root the discovered truth more firmly in the memory and to enflame the desire more keenly. Therefore by meditation we are taught the good and in contemplation we are confirmed in it. . . .

For that rest which prudence seeks for itself in meditation and describes by definitions, wisdom discovers in contemplation and lays hold on by experience. True prudence seeks and always ought to seek, the peace which Christ taught, that she be not troubled or afraid. She always enquires where such peace may be found and strives to defend her own security, but she always finds something in the past to sorrow for, something in the present to attack, something to watch against or fear in the future. So the soul may seek this peace eagerly with prudence and search it with subtle meditations but she will never find it except through wisdom and the grace of contemplation. But when the soul seeks to go forth from herself by the pure intelligence, and to enter wholly into that brightness of incorporeal light, she begins to experience from what these secret places have revealed to her, some inward sweetness and by it to build up her intelligence and transmute it into wisdom. Thus, in this ecstasy of mind, she will find that peace which is neither troubled nor afraid and she will gain that silence which is in heaven for the space of an half-hour, so that no tumult of conflicting thoughts shall disturb the spirit of contemplation and it shall find nothing to desire or ask for, no worry to decide, no hatreds to combat.

While at a certain point there is a unity in the mystical approach as it is made in the Eastern religions with that of Christianity, of late the two have sometimes been too facilely identified as constituting a "perennial philosophy". (Their distinctions have been well defined by Professor Zaehner in his book *Mysticism, Sacred and Profane*.[1]) There is a point of detachment which has often been accepted in the East as an end in itself, but which to the Christian mystic is only a beginning, the prerequisite for the state of sanctifying union that is his objective. Furthermore, whereas the Eastern mystic tends to regard inactivity as the primary demand of contemplation, the Christian mystic is pre-

[1]Oxford University Press, 1958.

pared to renounce inactivity itself when that renunciation is needful to his conforming to the will of God that has become his only motive. Christian history is peopled with saints who have been dependent upon unifying prayer as their source of grace yet have coupled it with lives of vast activity, an activity that might sometimes be properly described as superhuman in its tremendous service to mankind. Our Lord lived an active life, even an everyday kind of life that scandalized the Pharisees, as part of his life of intensive prayer. He did not condemn Martha for activity *per se* but for being "troubled about many things" and for a fussed absence of mind in his presence. We do not need to doubt that Mary engaged in the activities of the house when occasion called and such activity was God's will for her. Mysticism is constantly threatened by the excesses of quietism, and at times the need for the Church to check these excesses has had the effect of casting discredit upon the mystical way itself. But this mystical way needs to be recognized as simply the more concealed aspect of the demand made upon every Christian to live the Christ-life to the utmost of his bent, and the living of the Christ-life is not so much a modelling of ourselves upon Christ's life as a sharing of his apprehension of the divine will.

To the Christian therefore the essence of contemplation is neither religious rapture nor the pursuit of vision or miracle but simply the "putting on of Christ", the life of the constant practice of the will of God. All true prayer is a uniting of ourselves with his will, and the life of prayer is one that is led by many who might never in any way consider themselves "mystics" and whose practice of actual prayer might even seem in its outward form little like that described by mystical writers. Equally, there are those with both knowledge and apprehension of the mystical states who may themselves be fairly remote from the practice of this life in Christ.

It is one thing [says Richard of St Victor] to understand the depth of the mysteries by the intelligence alone and another to unfold them easily as often as you wish and to be able to explain them. See how few there are who are able to penetrate the mystical passages of the Scripture without the works and expositions of others and fewer still who desire to communicate their explanation by word or writing to the notice of others. Consider therefore, that as it seems to me, the gift of mystical understanding is one thing and the gift of mystical teaching another. Some excel in one, some in the other and some are remarkable in both things.

Richard of St Victor himself was not permitted to confine his life to his prayer, his writing, and his instruction of novices. His life also called for activity that was difficult, distracting, and painful to a lover of peace. In 1162 he was made prior of the abbey, and in the same year Ernisius, an Englishman, was elected abbot. Ernisius, unfortunately, proved unworthy of his office, wasting its resources, appointing favourites and absenting himself. He persecuted those who, like Richard, tried to maintain the spirit of their rule. Twice Ernisius was rebuked and warned by the Pope, but only after ten years was he at last deposed and a new abbot elected in his place. Richard, who had been compelled to protest at the conduct of his superior, just lived to see the abbey restored to happiness, dying, still a young man, in 1173.

Richard is one of the masters most closely drawn upon by the anonymous author of *The Cloud of Unknowing*, that beautiful introduction to prayer written in the Midland English dialect some two centuries after Richard's death. Early manuscript copies of his works survive in many parts of Europe, they must surely have reached his native Scotland too, but there no trace of them remains. They and their teaching were eradicated at the Reformation.

Nearly a hundred years after Richard's death there was born, reputedly at Maxton, between Melrose and Kelso, one of the greatest of Christian philosophers, John Duns Scotus. Becoming a Franciscan, Duns Scotus went to Oxford and Paris. In 1305 he was sent to Cologne, and died of the plague there at the early age of forty. Although his writings were mainly critical, and his style is involved and difficult, the brilliant intellect of Duns Scotus has left a lasting mark upon modern thought. Of all orthodox thinkers he is perhaps the only critic who made effective modification, chiefly in emphasizing the importance of the intuitive faculty, to the great scheme of Christian philosophy developed by St Thomas in the *Summa*. He was also a pioneer in upholding the doctrine of the Immaculate Conception, not accepted by Aquinas. Some of Duns Scotus's ideas were taken up by the earlier Reformers, but, better understood, were put to effective account by the Counter-Reformation in the sixteenth century, when the revulsion of the English Reformers gave rise to a curious etymological freak by which a man possessed, by any standards, of a superb intellect, gave his name to be a synonym of stupidity—"dunce"!

In later mediaeval days a number of Scottish names occur amongst those Carmelites active in the efforts that were made to reform the order from the laxity that ravaged it before the Reformation, although these efforts were not finally successful until the great days of St Teresa and St John of the Cross in the sixteenth century.

The decline in spirituality that overtook the monastic orders generally in the later Middle Ages was due in part to changing conditions, the spiralling of the human upheaval that brings now one, now another aspect of man's potential raw and hungry to time's daylight. Human society like the individual himself demands a multifarious development, and changing aspects of growth are natural to both. Yet man is always at his worst when he loses his spiritual vision because his attention is too set upon material things or concerned with a vain intellectuality. Now that the upheaval of the Reformation is falling into perspective, and we are better able to distinguish loss from gain, it may be that we shall make fresh progress in the sphere that man can least afford to allow to fall into neglect and contempt.

CHAPTER VI

POETRY

AT present the last Scot in whom sanctity has received formal recognition is St Gilbert who died in 1245. He was Bishop of Caithness, a wealthy man who gave his money for the building of Dornoch Cathedral, and a humble one who helped with his own hands in the building and ran a glassworks for the making of glass for the windows. A portion of a broken statue is all that remains of his tomb, once a place of pilgrimage for the honouring of virtue in the north. Of course, the Church's formal recognition of sanctity is not exclusive, it does not imply that there are not many other souls as holy; the formal recognition of particular saints is made for the benefit of the rest of us in such times and places as it may be of help to have exemplars of different aspects of the Christian life. Yet certain periods produce considerable numbers of avowed saints.

The first thirty-five Popes were all canonized. But this is not to be put down merely to early enthusiasm in acclaiming sanctity. The process was less formal in those days. Local bishops could pronounce canonization, which might stem from strong popular demand. Some earlier haloes may carry less weight, even so we must remember that the young Church demanded a higher standard of its members, not because it was a better Church but because it was a far less comfortable one. Most of the early Popes had very short reigns, many of which ended abruptly in martyrdom. Heroic sanctity was the usual demand made upon Christians. There was rarely any other reason for coming into the Church than the right one, and that on a high level of integrity and courage. But by the time whole countries were Christian, the Church in her members was inevitably diluted: many were there for little reason beyond the fact that they had been born to

Christian parents. Later again the Church offered means of worldly advancement, and she suffered for long centuries from careerist and political churchmen, who at different times and in different places might dominate much of her outward life.

But this "dilution" of corporate Christianity is tragic only in so far as man's fallen state makes its evils inevitable. The Church must insist upon certain rules for those who wish to be her practising members, but she can only work within those rules and if she were to reject a man simply because he was a sinner she would fail in the mission of her Founder who came "not to save the just but to save sinners". We can never forget that the first human being our Lord welcomed into his kingdom—"This day thou shalt be with me in paradise"—was a self-confessed sinner. Indeed, the only difference of which we are told between the two condemned thieves who suffered with Christ at Golgotha was that one admitted his guilt and the other did not. At first both had rebuked him that he would not save them from death. But then the penitent cried out that while they had received only the due reward of their deeds, Christ had "done no evil", and appealed to our Lord to remember him when he came into his kingdom.

It was not a virtuous life that earned the thief redemption, only some strand of aspiration in his life that found expression at the end when he freely confessed himself a sinner and in faith asked God's forgiveness. It was humility before the Godhead that opened to him the salvation for the giving of which Christ was even then suffering his most terrible agony.

Only by this acknowledgement of his own smallness and shame can man be exalted in God. Great poets who may also be substantial sinners owe their merit, not to their sins, but to the keenness of their apprehension of a state of wholeness and holiness, the state personified in Christ himself. Implicitly their pain is that of St Paul who complained that while his soul knew and sought the good, his body lusted after what was evil. In France the gaolbird, François Villon, and in Scotland the one time "feigned friar", William Dunbar, reach from delectation in earthy abasement to a vision of purity that redeems the body as well as the soul. Each of them turns from a world of harlots and pimps to look with longing devotion towards

> the rose Mary, flower of floweris,
> The clear sun whom no cloud devouris.

These were men in whom failure to achieve an ideal never led to a denial, or even to a modification of that ideal: they are sinners, but confessed and, for all their failure, reluctant sinners. "Penance did walk the house within", to quote Dunbar again. Their philosophy is totally different from that of those who, faced with their own inability to approach the ideal, seek to reduce love to a mere gloss upon animal instincts and the whole challenge of life to a lukewarm aspiration or a nebulous aestheticism. Even when they write of wickedness with relish and rash delectation they do not commit the cardinal sin of justifying it and presenting it as man's true good.

William Dunbar, born about 1460, became a Franciscan novice and travelled in England and France . . .

> In freiris weid full fairly have I fleichit
> In it I haif in pulpit gon and preichit. . . .
> As lang as I did beir the freiris style
> In me, God wot, was mony wrink and wyle,
> In me was falset with every wicht to flatter,
> Which mycht be flemit with na haly watter,
> I was ay ready all men to begyle.

In 1501 he was in London, probably in connection with James IV's marriage to Margaret, sister of Henry VIII, and thereafter remained at the Scottish Court. He had left the Franciscan order but was ordained a secular priest by 1504, after which he constantly asked the king for a benefice, but instead of giving him one James increased his pension, preferring to keep him as Court poet. After James's death at Flodden in 1513 we hear no more of Dunbar, and he perhaps at last received his benefice as it seems on the whole unlikely that he went to Flodden.

As Court poet Dunbar entertained the king with verses about life in the Palace and amongst the Edinburgh citizens. He played off courtliness with crudeness, seeing the grotesqueness of the human condition beneath its silks and pretences and celebrating their conjunction in forceful but sophisticated verse.

Modern critics sometimes write as though mediaeval poets such as Dunbar wrote of religion as a mere formality, a set of symbols or conventions convenient to their poetic expression. Even although such critics are not themselves poets one might have expected them to appreciate better the way in which the poetic genius works. When Dunbar writes of the dance of the seven deadly sins through hell he may do so with brutal relish, but whatever of symbol he may use he knows the bitter reality that it contains: whatever the form of his poetic diction it is fired by the urgency of a valid inspiration. Hell is reality to him, he knows it as an inexpressible horror, symbolized in his poem in acceptable terms but remaining an entity beyond man's expression, a ghastliness that he can only dimly visualize. Yet that dim vision is enough to perturb him fiercely, or, more calmly, faced by the choice allowed:

> What is this lyfe but ane straucht way to deid,
> Whilk has a tyme to pass and nane to dwell;
> A sliding while us lent to seek remeid,
> A free chois given to paradice or hell,
> A prey to deid, whom vain is to repell;
> A short torment for infineit glaidnes,
> As short ane joy for lestand hevynes.

And again, in his *Lament for the Makars* (poets):

> Our plesance here is all vain glory,
> This fals world is but transitory,
> The flesh is bruckle, the Fiend is sle:
> *Timor mortis conturbat me.*

This is no playing with words or idling with ideas but born of the poet's struggle to put words to the truth that seizes him. For, howsoever confined many of its avenues, poetry is of its essence an apprehension of the inexpressible, of the limits of the human mind and human words, an effort to enrich and to sidetrack them by the use of sound, allusion, allegory and every device that may enable man to burst through their constriction. The poet tries to convey in words what he knows cannot be said by words, and most inexpressible of all things to us are the attributes of God, so that these are always, advertently or inadvertently, the highest aspiration of poetry.

When he writes his hymns of triumph in the birth and resurrection of our Lord, Dunbar's words evoke the liturgy and the sound of sacred music as vehicle for the intensity of his feeling in these, appropriately the finest of his poems:

> Sinners, be glad and penance do
> And thank your maker hairtfully,
> For he that ye micht not come to
> To you is cummin fully humbly;
> Your saulis with his blood to buy
> And lowse you of the Fiend's arrest,
> And only of his own mercy:
> *Pro nobis puer natus est.*

And, again:

> Done is a battell on the dragon black,
> Our campioun Christ confoundet has his force;
> The yettis of hell are broken with a crack,
> The sign triumphal raisit is of the croce,
> The divillis trymmillis with hideous voce,
> The saulis are borrowit and to the bliss can go,
> Christ with his blood our ransomis does indoce:
> *Surrexit dominus de sepulchro.*

A gentler and subtler poet than Dunbar is Robert Henryson. He was an older man and died in time to be included in Dunbar's "Lament". His Fables are full of charming humour with delightful observation of nature and a peaceful world: days when

> Sweet was the smell of flouris, white and reid,
> The noyes of birdis richt delitious . . .

or evenings on which

> The nicht was licht, and penny full the moon.

They are much the most attractive verse fables in the language.

> Upon ane tyme (as Esope could report)
> Ane litill Mouse came till ane River syde;
> She micht not wade, her schankis were sa short,

> She could not swim, she had na horse to ride:
> Of veray force behovit her to bide,
> And to and fro beside that River deep
> She ran, cryand with mony piteous peep.

As Edwin Muir has observed there is an ease in such narration
that belongs to the golden days of mediaeval Scotland, an
acceptance of life with its pains and joys distinct from the fervour,
bitterness and triumph of Dunbar. The beautiful *Testament of
Cresseid* is, again, handled in a manner quite unlike Dunbar's.
Here is no gloating, or even lingering over Cresseid's shame or
the ravages of her leprosy. The whole poem is an essay in compassion, like the epitaph Troilus writes for the tomb of his dead
love:

> Lo, fair Ladyeis, Crisseid, of Troyis toun,
> Sumtyme countit the flower of Womanheid,
> Under this stane, late Lipper, lyis deid.

The poet writes not as one re-telling a legend but of a real girl
whose fate concerns him personally; while her gods are Venus
and Cupid, it is in Christian terms, universal in their application,
that he sees that fate. She is not the victim of the stern revengeful
God who for centuries after Henryson's time dominates so much
Scottish thought. Her suffering is not the work of revenge but of
redemption: a redemption expressed in the mute reconciliation
with Troilus that she finds at the point of death. Indeed, it is
strange that Henryson should ever have been charged with
moralizing in *The Testament*, for the greatness of the poem lies
just in the fact that he does not moralize, the ineluctable Moral
Law is implicit, the poet never needs to step outside his creation
to pass judgment. Even his formal signing off seems to cast aside
all recrimination:

> Sen she is deid, I speik of her no more.

The author of *The Testament* is, we feel, a fully integrated man,
one who needs to set up neither as moralist nor, in revolt, as
immoralist, because he has subjugated the vagaries of his own
judgment to the actuality of God's. In this Henryson touches the
heights of Dante and of Shakespeare, and his *Testament* deserved

to be printed, as it was in early times, as the conclusion to Chaucer's *Troilus and Cresseide*, providing, in Sir Herbert Grierson's words, "a real catharsis leaving us at peace with Cresseid as Chaucer's poem scarcely does".

Of Henryson's life we know next to nothing save that he was a schoolmaster, presumably a monk, at the Benedictine Abbey of Dunfermline: it was a Grammar and Song School, but Henryson's association must have been with the former, for we have his own admission:

> Of sic musick to write I do but dote
> Therefore at this matter a straw I lay
> For in my lyfe I could never syng a note.

Not that, being poet rather than scholar, he lays great claim to learning:

> In hamelie language and in termes rude
> Me neidis wryte, for why of Eloquence
> Nor Rethoricke, I never understude.

But he was well versed in the Classics, besides being a profound admirer of Chaucer.

His "hamelie language" came nearer to Anglo-Saxon than the more Normanized language in which Chaucer had written a hundred years earlier. Middle Scots was a variant of the Northern English dialect and was gradually replacing Gaelic in the Lowlands since St Margaret had established the southern speech as the language of the Court—although the mother-tongue of Walter Kennedy with whom Dunbar had a friendly poetic duel was, since he was an Ayrshire man, still the Gaelic. Dunbar refers to Gaelic as "Irysshe" and to Middle Scots as "Inglis", although Gavin Douglas a few years later differentiates between the Scots and English languages. To some degree, of course, the language the makars used was a literary one, although no doubt their application of it enriched the popular usage, since poets in their struggle with words give them new graces and potentials. Gavin Douglas was the first poet in either Scotland or England to make a metrical translation of a Classical author. His translation of Virgil's *Aeneid* is remarkably good although he is sometimes diffusive and, hard put to it to find appropriate words, has to coin new ones from Latin or French metal, many of which coinages were never taken up. But, of course, Scots as a literary language was soon to receive a *quietus*.

It is in the prologues to the various books of the *Aeneid* that Gavin Douglas gives us sidelights upon his own life and times. They range from a poet's enjoyment of the sensate world—such as the May sunrise:

> And al small fowlys singis on the spray
> Welcum the lord of lycht, and lamp of day

—to bitter comment upon sad and sinister times:

> Quhat wickitness, quhat wanthrift now in warld warkis.

In fact much of his life was devoured by the evil of the day; the confusion and corruption that, largely owing to the country's tragic succession of royal minorities, bedevilled Scottish politics with factious noblemen. A churchman who was also a member of the powerful, scheming Douglas family, he was for years involved in jockeying for power and position. John Lesley, Bishop of Ross, the Scottish historian who lived not long after, remarked of him, "If he had not mixed himself up with the national tumults, he would have been truly worthy of being consecrated in the writings and memory of all, on account of his fragrant wit and singular erudition".

Not that Gavin Douglas was a man of gross ambition. During the short time that he was able to occupy his See of Dunkeld he proved a better bishop than most of his contemporaries. In the violent affray between the Douglas faction and the Hamiltons in the streets of Edinburgh, known to history as "Cleanse the Causeway", Gavin Douglas played the part of a mediator. When James Beaton, Archbishop of Glasgow, protested to him, "There is no remedy, upon my conscience I cannot help what is about to happen", striking his breast so that the coat of mail beneath his vestments rattled, Gavin Douglas dryly remarked: "How now, my lord, methinks your conscience clatters!" He then went off to pray for peace, but after the Hamiltons were routed and the Archbishop was taken from the sanctuary he had sought behind the high altar of the church of the Blackfriars, it was the

Bishop of Dunkeld who saved him from summary execution.

But it was hardly possible to mingle in the hideous politics of the day without tarnish, or at least a dissipation of talent and usefulness. Gavin Douglas became involved in the fringes of plot and counterplot, the machinations of James IV's unscrupulous widow, Margaret Tudor, and of her second husband, the Earl of Angus. Bishops had turned politicians, or it might be more apt to say, natural politicians became bishops for the sake of the power and money the position gave them. Gavin Douglas himself went into exile in London where he died of the plague in 1522 in his forty-eighth year, revered amongst the scholars and poets there.

Scotland was entering upon her most tragic days, her own corner of that general tragedy of Christendom. Inevitable change and conflict lay ahead. The question was whether reform of the Church's administration could be achieved in time to prevent a chaos of destruction. But abuses within the Church were also the vested interests of laymen. In Scotland the commendatory system had been introduced in the reign of James III enabling the king and others to appoint lay abbots, men whose only interest was in the accumulated wealth of the abbeys and to whom any reforms that might threaten their enjoyment of such wealth were heartily to be resisted. With papal sanction, James V appointed five of his bastard sons to the richest abbacies in the country. Such men were naturally opposed to administrative reform and as naturally enthusiastic for a revolution that would make them absolute possessors of property to which otherwise they could only claim the life-rent, and that with certain conditions and expenses attached: their convictions were patently neither spiritual nor intellectual. The most honest and disinterested criticism came from a handful of priests and monks, men such as Archbishop Forman, Quintin Kennedy and Ninian Winzet, for these were men who felt bitterly the failure of their fellow clergy to live the life they proclaimed. Criticism then, it may be remarked, was free and open: both Dunbar and Henryson make it. Sir David Lindsay of the Mount, the last of the makars, was a more reckless critic. As a poet he is a minor figure but in his *Satire of the Three Estates* Lindsay achieved a rambling but powerful drama that compares

The Sacrament of Extreme Unction
The sole surviving panel of a fifteenth-century retable from an
Edinburgh church depicting the Seven Sacraments. Found
amongst foundations off Edinburgh High St. (National Museum
of Antiquities of Scotland)

Photo: Malcolm Murray

St Matthew

St Mark

St Luke

St John

The Four Evangelists
from the MS. of St Margaret's Gospels in the Bodleian Library,
Oxford

favourably with anything written in England at the time. Criticism of the Church in the *Satire* is lavish, but rash in its tendency, too readily inspiring an emotional and witless revulsion. It was performed three times, before James V and his queen at Linlithgow and again after her husband's death before the queen in Edinburgh. Mary of Guise was a devout Catholic and it is plain that she did not shun criticism of clerical abuse. Unfortunately, although he himself never actually apostatized, Lindsay gave ammunition to the Church's enemies for that final revolt that was to sweep away so much more than clerical abuses, to sweep away the arts themselves so that Lindsay's own play was never again to be performed for four hundred years, when it was revived at the Edinburgh Festival, and, oddly enough, acted in the Assembly Hall of the Church of Scotland which happens to stand on the actual site of the palace of Mary of Guise.

It is interesting that after Chaucer himself the best of the "Chaucerians" should be Scots. Yet whereas poetry in England thereafter went from strength to strength, in Scotland it almost died out completely. For one thing, the Reformation brought an abrupt linguistic break. Middle Scots came to be identified with the Catholic interest, whereas John Knox with his English affiliation spoke "Suddrons" (he was accused by Ninian Winzet of having forgotten his mother-tongue), and introduced English Bibles and very inferior English versions of the Psalms. Then again literature that was not of a heavily pious or fiercely propagandist nature was firmly discouraged as being frivolous and unworthy of the attention of the elect. The only one of the makars whose work was freely published in the post-Reformation period was Lindsay; although not very distinguished as poetry it was encouraged for its abuse of the Auld Kirk. The theatre, of course, was for long entirely proscribed. Only amongst the humbler people did the making of ballads continue; and the ballads from the Scottish Border and as far north as Aberdeenshire retained a distinctive national quality that gives them a unique place in ballad literature. In the dwindling Gaelic-speaking districts that remained for long largely outside the influence of Calvinism, song and poetry survived better.

E

CHAPTER VII

DISUNION

"IT is we bishops who are most responsible for all the evils now burdening the flock of Christ. . . . We cannot even name any other cause than ourselves. . . . If God punished us as we deserved, we should have been long since as Sodom and Gomorrah." So spoke Cardinal Pole on behalf of the legates at the Council of Trent on January 7th, 1546.

Nobody can question the acute need for reform that faced the Church at the beginning of the sixteenth century. The only question was what nature the reform should take. Again and again throughout its history the need for reform of the Church's leaders and institutions had arisen. Again and again, although it might often seem tardily, the need had been met. The great social and intellectual changes that we group under the heading of the Renaissance had certainly brought new problems whose solution Pope and bishops, absorbed in politics or sunk in luxury, had manifestly refused to face, despite the complaints and warnings of good men.

It is in the nature of historical writing to over-simplify, to trace trends and movements to what is often thereafter called their inevitable outcome. There is always danger of distortion in such a process: wisdom after the event is more easy than necessarily wise. The very simple picture often presented in popular Protestant histories of mankind growing to a new emancipation that flowered at last in the Reformation is one that is dispelled by even a little knowledge of the events of the time. With it goes the idea that the Reformation saw the institution of private judgment in matters of religion. However much at the beginning of their careers Luther and Calvin may have exhorted the individual to judge for himself, both brought their reforms to fruition by clamping down upon it severely. Each found it necessary to impose his own judgment firmly upon "liberated" humanity, to make of himself a very private pope independent of tradition or correction, and the world has perhaps hardly seen a community so completely subjected to an authority that claimed control even over its most personal and spiritual life as Calvin's theocratic state of Geneva. Calvin actually resorted to the system of families spying upon their own members that has become so powerful a weapon against individual freedom in the authoritarian states of today. Even under Lutheran rule it availed nothing to the citizen arrested and brought before the Council who "kept on saying that we have no power to compel the citizens to go to the sermon against their conscience, since in the beginning of these changes we particularly said that no man had the power to lord it over our conscience". It was imposed by Law that men should not only attend the sermon but should believe every word of it. One need hardly add that the preacher's private judgment might make greater and more arbitrary demands than the dogma of the Church.

Equally unfounded is the idea that the Reformation was the outcome of popular uprisings. Commonly it was imposed by prince or government; Scotland is perhaps the only country or state that may be said to have made the change in opposition to the will of its ruler, who was out of the country at the time. In England all the popular risings were on behalf of the old faith, and were very bloodily put down.

But to dispose of common fallacies concerning the Reformation by recourse to historical fact is not to deny the lamentable state of the Catholic Church in those days. Nor, even if the characters of the leading figures amongst the Reformers do not stand up well to scrutiny: Luther with his declining integrity and increasing opportunism, Calvin with his polished brain and dead heart, or such a minor figure outside his own country as the coarse and sanctimonious John Knox: is there any questioning the genuine motives that moved many thinking people to inquire whether there were not grave errors in the doctrine of a Church whose state had fallen so low. The open concubinage of bishops and abbots, the illiteracy of lesser priests, the draining away of money from every nation to maintain the notorious splendour of Rome; all seemed little linked with the life of Christ. It was easy to grow doubtful and to forget that the Law might be valid even although its guardians proved wretchedly weak and fallible in their own lives, easy to overlook the relevant text in the new vernacular Bibles, Christ's own judgment on the same situation when he castigated the Scribes and Pharisees yet exhorted his hearers to observe the Law that they taught while repudiating the example of their lives. It was easy again, when so many monks led vicious, or at least idle lives, to forget the lesson of the great founders of the Religious Orders who in promulgating their Rules knew the winnowing and proving required of humankind before it can hope to live the "simple" Christ-life. Amongst the more illiterate especially, countless religious enthusiasts bursting with a sense of revelation set themselves up as prophets of re-formed Christianity, assuming their very ignorance identified them with the simple faith of the Age of the Apostles.

These enthusiasts were generally referred to as Anabaptists. They had no organization or common authority, indeed their creed tended to prevent this, being determinedly one of private revelation, their claim a personal divine inspiration. Such eccentrics had existed long before the Reformation. In a time of social stability their excesses might be laughed at, overlooked and forgotten. But in the upheaval of the Reformation the anarchy they portended caused them to be burnt or otherwise put to death in great numbers by Catholic and Protestant rulers alike. Although the great rising of the German peasants was not primarily religious, but a revolt against intolerable servitude, Anabaptists and more orthodox Protestants were largely involved. Luther at first supported them, but when the princes, so much more important than peasants to his cause, banded together against them, he wrote his tract urging the princes to "kill them, strangle them; what else is to be done to the mad dog that leaps at you? Strike, throttle, stab, secretly or openly." Years after he claimed all the credit for the slaughter of 100,000 peasants: "It was I who slew all the peasants in the insurrection, for it was I who com-

manded them to be slaughtered; their blood is on my head. . . .
But I throw the responsibility on our Lord God who instructed
me to give this order."

No, Luther's reputation as liberator of the oppressed will not
stand, and his private interpretation of God's will clearly does not
tally with Christian revelation. As Ronald Knox wrote of the
Scottish minister of a hundred years later whose sermon on the
Amalekites inspired the massacre of the Episcopalian prisoners at
Philiphaugh, "That is the worst of it; the ultrasupernaturalist
faced with a moral problem believes that the solution is given him
directly by the voice of God, and from that arbitrament there is
no appeal." Calvin's creed of predestination, which through the
agency of John Knox ultimately became the doctrine of the
Scottish Reformation, in particular tended to "ultrasupernaturalism". Calvin's claim was that God had already decided on the
salvation or damnation of each individual soul and nothing that
man might do himself could change his destination in heaven or
hell. Despite the external austerity of Presbyterian ritual, in-
transigent human emotion played its inevitable part, none the
less potent for being concealed. The doctrinaire Calvinist custo-
marily felt—he could have no other evidence than his feeling—
that he himself was one of the elect. It was a feeling liable to be
charged with the force of pent-up passion, inclining him to feel
with equal certainty that those who disagreed with him must be
bound for hell, and, being therefore created by God only for
immolation, they could claim no Christian charity and anything
that eradicated them from the face of the earth was a godly deed.
Of course this dark creed gradually lost force, even although it
remains the official doctrine of Presbyterianism, but for long it
inspired a rough courage that carried the Covenanters to their
martyr's deaths confidently calling down hellfire upon the
Episcopalian heads of their persecutors.

For Luther salvation was the reward of faith, and of faith alone.
To him the Epistle of St James was "an epistle of straw" because
James had written: "Thou believest that there is one God. Thou
dost well; the devils also believe and tremble. But wilt thou know,
O vain man, that faith without works is dead?"

Protestantism has come a long way from the creeds of those principally responsible for its doctrines. If such figures as Luther and Calvin and Knox are commemorated today it is perhaps rather for the sake of sentiment than out of desire to endorse the doctrines they actually held, for the emphasis has generally shifted from faith to good works as the means of salvation, and the faith that is held very often takes the form less of an intellectual assent than of an emotional acceptance of what in the Christian creed the believer feels to be true.

Great and complex differences mark the Reformation in the different countries in which it was brought about. In many ways the English Reformation is outside the main stream at least as far as doctrine is concerned. Although the Reformation there was directly the result of the matrimonial instability of Henry VIII, and he was the first head of the Church of England, those Protestant historians who allege that he was a schismatic Catholic rather than a Protestant have a good case to make. Even although he allowed Lutheranism to be disseminated when it suited his politics, Henry himself detested it. His henchman and shameless collaborator in the dissolution of the English monasteries, Thomas Cromwell, although eulogized in Foxe's *Book of Martyrs* as of the purest Protestant orthodoxy, died on the scaffold proclaiming himself a Catholic. The real hero of the English Reform is Elizabeth's great statesman, William Cecil, Lord Burghley, who more than any other single individual established Protestantism in his own country. He was not notably a religious man, and we may reasonably regard his primary motives as political and patriotic. Equally, this extraordinarily successful and unscrupulous statesman, who never failed in any important project he undertook, perhaps deserves, more than any other individual, the credit for the establishment of Protestantism as the state religion of the separate Kingdom of Scotland. It was no mean achievement for one man.

The Scottish cardinal David Beaton is the key figure to the days just before the Reformation took effect. Supporting first James V, then his widowed Queen Mary of Lorraine, he assiduously and successfully foiled the efforts of Henry VIII to extend his reform and his power to Scotland. Beaton is recognized even by Protestant historians as one of the greatest and most patriotic of all Scottish statesmen. If it is argued that his support of the French alliance was made more attractive to him personally by the gift of a wealthy French benefice, the single-mindedness of his statesmanship remains all too rare in our history. Moreover, France was an ally, not always loyal but in no sense an acquisitive enemy. England on the other hand, the "auld enemy", laid claim to overlordship, and her statesmen were constantly working to weaken or destroy the internal government of the country. Those therefore who accepted English bribes and acted in her cause were traitors; if some of them acted in part for ideological reasons, these were still quislings. George Wishart, an attractive but unscrupulous character, whose burning for heresy was subsequently used as an excuse for committing the murder, was himself already, as English state documents confirm, an active go-between in the English plot to murder Beaton. The cardinal may have had knowledge of this, and it is a pity that Wishart had not been put to death for his treachery rather than his beliefs. Although Cardinal Beaton came to be represented as a monster of persecution, he compares favourably with many statesmen of his day and after in having burnt only seven heretics, and never resorting to additional torture. The worst that can be alleged against him concerns his private life; we are not allowed to forget his legitimation of ten bastards. But his life and conduct may fairly be compared with that of his post-Reformation successors amongst Scottish statesmen; with the Earl of Morton, a man quite grotesquely vicious, habitual seducer, murderer, swindler and traitor; with the Earl of Moray, scheming for the Throne, building his private fortune without scruple, lick-spittle to Elizabeth and Cecil, the chief architect by constant treachery of the ruin of his queen and half-sister; with Maitland of Lethington, whose persistent career of double-dealing lacks even the patriotism that redeems that of Cecil, and seems at times quite pointlessly tortuous.

It was Voltaire, no friend to the priesthood, who observed that however low at particular times in history priests may have sunk, their conduct as a whole is always somewhat better than that of their lay contemporaries. Moreover, although the complexities of Scottish politics and the feuds between the great families increasingly vitiated the lives of prelates, we should not forget the debt that we still owe to many of blameless life: such men as Bishop Turnbull who founded Glasgow University, Bishop Elphinstone who brought serene goodness and wisdom to his activities as statesman and diplomat and founded the University at Aberdeen besides bringing the first printing-press to Scotland, and to his worthy successor, Gavin Dunbar, who completed the building of St Machar's Cathedral. Even the youngest of the Scottish Universities, that of Edinburgh, although only established, and then with difficulty, after the Reformation, was the endowment of another blameless Catholic bishop, Robert Reid.

As it has been written, habitually with strong bias, Scottish history sometimes seems to suggest that the essential character of the nation and its institutions is vested in the Reformation. This would be to give us, for a unit of Western Europe, a short history indeed, and to overlook much the greater part of our history as a nation, to treat Malcolm Canmore, Wallace and Bruce as figures in a romantic pageant, linked to us by little more than sentiment. The Reformation is only an incident, if a major one, in the long story of Scotland. While it profoundly influences the centuries to follow, in its turn it owes much of its nature to the immediately preceding centuries, a period in which, although there were many brighter aspects, political instability oppressed much of Scottish life. This left a bitterness and frustration that turned to a puritanical creed as something that offered justification and a dour stability. An extraordinary series of royal minorities was the primary cause of Scotland's weakness. Although for the most part men exceptionally able, one after another the Stewart kings died young, leaving minors or mere children to succeed them. The noble families warred and conspired against each other for the power that never came firmly into the royal hands, and in the process became increasingly unscrupulous, predatory, and ultimately mere hirelings of an enemy whose constant concern was the preventing of a united Scotland. It was to the king that the common people looked for protection and justice. Loyalty to the Stewart cause was grounded in past benefits: it was no servility, the "sturdy democracy" with which Scots are commonly credited goes back long before the Reformation.

Clearly, it owed its origins to the geography of Scotland: the fact that the country has no large area of flat country but is divided up in all directions by ranges of hills, and in many by inlets of the sea, a factor that if it tended to foster disunity also made for an independence and love of freedom that left its mark strongly in the character even of the humble and poor. We get an echo of this, and one remarkable in any country for its time, in the protest voiced not by the nobles but by lesser men against the claims of Edward I to the overlordship of Scotland. In 1320 it rings out clearly in the splendid words of the Declaration of Independence written on behalf of the Scottish people by the Prior of Arbroath. In it the Parliament of Scotland maintains, referring to King Robert the Bruce:

> To him we are obliged and resolved to adhere in all things, both on account of his rights and of his merits as the man who has restored the people's safety, and will defend their freedom. But if he should turn aside from the work he has begun, wishing that we or our kingdom should be subjected to the King or people of England, we will immediately endeavour to expel him as our enemy and the subverter of his own rights and ours, and will make another king to defend us. For so long as a mere hundred of us shall stand, we will never surrender to the dominion of England. What we fight for is not glory nor wealth nor honour: but freedom, that no good man yields save with his life.

This letter, addressed to Pope John XXII, gained papal recognition of Scottish independence. Compared with the clarity and dignity of the words of the Prior of Arbroath, putting forward the claim of mankind not for licence but for that liberty of circumstance in which his spirit may find its life, John Knox's talk of liberty is merely the dubious and factious oratory of the demagogue, and all too often anticipates the cant that has served to introduce totalitarian tyrannies of today.

Knox's chief work, his *History of the Reformation*, is propaganda in which he is little concerned with truth but throws wild and often quite unsubstantiated accusations and abuse at all those with whom he disagrees, while being servilely prepared to condone the vice of those who support his cause. Written with a fine barbaric vigour, its pithy hypocrisy would be more amusing had it not for so long been given serious respect by many Scots possessed of a far greater personal integrity than its author. It is a kind of brain-washing, noisily crying scandal, especially as regards sexual vice, to cover up the deficiencies in the Reformers' case. Whether Knox's own sexual life was beyond criticism has often been disputed, but he is revealed more certainly in his own words as the self-enthralled victim of a twisted and malignant mentality. No doubt he started life as a "mixed-up kid", and the adversity he brought upon himself as a young man confirmed him in this unhappy state; but such unfortunates do much evil and are certainly not wholesome national heroes, even when heavily whitewashed. David Hume credits Knox with being the initiator in Scotland of the "fanaticism and hypocrisy which long infected that kingdom". Yet a certain shrillness of declamation is perhaps natural to priests like John Knox who, rather than reform their lives in accordance with their promise, reform their promise to accord with their lives.

Just as the Scottish State was oppressed, chaotic and corrupt at the beginning of the sixteenth century, like evil beset her Church. The appointment of laymen as abbots, and even as bishops, helped to frustrate all attempts to promote reform from within, while many of the priests, although by no means all, were illiterate and ill-instructed. Even so, under the rule of James V, although he himself aggravated the abuses, Scotland held out against Protestant reform. Even after the confusion that followed his death, during the forlorn regency of Mary of Guise, a compromise might well have been reached whereby men would have been allowed to hold which faith they wished had it not been for Knox, Moray and their caucus and, even more, for the mastermind of Cecil and the power of England behind them.

In May 1559 John Knox launched his campaign in earnest

with the sack of the churches in Perth, and the next month saw the destruction of the Cathedral of St Andrews. No doubt the fabric of many churches was in a state of neglect before the Reformation, and many more were allowed to decay and collapse after it, but John Knox initially, although later he tried to shift the blame upon his "rascal multitude", exulted over the deliberate witless destruction of much of the finest art and architecture our country has ever seen.

The next year the inconoclasts were assisted by an English army and the beautiful abbeys of Dunfermline, Kelso and Melrose were added to the ruins. On June 10th Mary of Guise died, after being insulted even on her deathbed by one of the poor fanatic preachers whose ultrasupernaturalism recognized no bounds of decency or respect. The young Queen of Scots was still in France, but in August 1560 the Scottish Estates met and, although they had no power to do so without a royal assent that was never granted, established the Reformed religion and made it compulsory upon her people.

CHAPTER VIII

VICTIM

ON August 19th, 1561, Mary Stuart returned to Scotland. Her ship came into the Firth of Forth in a dense fog, which, said some of the Frenchmen aboard, "boded that we were now to land in a quarrelsome, mischief-making, unpleasant kingdom", while on land John Knox boded "sorrow, dolour, darkness and all impiety. . . . That forewarning God gave to us!" It was true, he had reason to know, he fully intended it; but he preferred to see his foresight as the gift of prophecy.

As the queen rode from Leith to Holyrood some young men petitioned her for their own lives and for that of a friend whom they had rescued from hanging for taking the part of Robin Hood in a May Day festival, all such customs having come under the lethal ban of the Reform. Mary pardoned them, and her act of grace and mercy gave immediate grounds for the preachers to call her a harlot, so establishing a precedent still followed by many of their heirs.

Within a week or two Knox secured his first interview, and went to Holyrood with a mouthful of foul words to hurl at a girl of nineteen, not long a widow, who was faced with the appalling problem of bringing peace to a corrupt and factious State. Even although we have only his own account of his interviews, Mary's replies are remarkable for their wisdom and patience. Had he been less insensate, Knox would not have recorded as much of them as he did, for he never hesitated to suppress facts that he could see were damaging to his case. He gloried in the fact that in one interview he made the poor girl weep; but she did not weep for shame in the face of righteousness, as he liked to suppose, but rather with frustration in the face of crassness. To the dispassionate mind Knox's words are simply brutal and bad-mannered, attributes that spring from motives very different from Christian integrity. One cannot help suspecting that some confusion between mere bad manners and fearless honesty was established for his countrymen by Knox. Actually, of course, he had nothing to fear, he was fully supported by, in fact was merely the noisy tool of, Mary's leading statesmen.

It is at least generally agreed that Moray, Morton and Lethington and their confederates amongst Mary's statesmen were as tortuously corrupt a set of noblemen as may be found grouped together anywhere in history. Since Mary herself has had more books written about her than any other queen who ever reigned, the story has been often told, if not usually with any conscientious reference to the ascertainable facts which in Mary's case are particularly well documented. David Rizzio, for example, is regularly depicted as a young and dashing Italian, whereas he was in fact rather elderly and notably ill-favoured, but he was an honest man and a loyal servant. He was deliberately hacked down in front of the queen when she was six months gone with child. Even before the murder the English ambassador was writing to Cecil hinting that it was hoped that the queen might die at the same time; and John Knox was preparing the way by justifying murder from the pulpit of St Giles. The rebel lords were still uncertain what to do with her, and with violence and insult held her captive after Rizzio's death, while the people of Edinburgh threatened to come to the rescue of the queen whom, despite all slander, they still loved and had good reason to love. Mary persuaded the craven Darnley to help her to escape, which utterly broke up the rebellion for the time being. John Knox himself scurried out of Edinburgh.[1] In the security of the Castle Mary gave birth to her son: the only royalty of her day whose descendant retains her throne. It was there that the plotters revealed to her Darnley's betrayal of her cause and his part in Rizzio's murder. They hinted to her that Darnley might be

[1]As Dr Warr points out in *The Presbyterian Tradition*, whenever he had reason to fear for his safety John Knox made himself very scarce. Dr Warr refers more than once to Knox's "besetting cowardice", and it seems odd that he should still regard such a man as a hero: "the Hero of Scottish Protestantism".

liquidated. She forbade anything evil to be done. None the less, they plotted the death of this confederate who had also betrayed them.

There were two separate plots that took effect at Kirk o' Field. To the gunpowder plot Darnley himself was surely privy, for he had made secret arrangements to leave the house at five in the morning, and the gunpowder was not put under his bedroom, which was undamaged, but under the *salle* where Mary would have been had she not gone back to Holyrood. Although the ramifications of Kirk o' Field are never now likely to be fully unravelled, it is at least not unreasonably argued that this was a Catholic plot to get rid of Mary because of her refusal to persecute the Protestants. Meanwhile the Confederate Lords had signed a band with Bothwell that Darnley should die and he should marry the queen; and it was he or his servants who murdered Darnley as he tried to escape through the garden actually before the house was blown up.

Although with suspicious celerity English agents at once started a campaign to implicate her, the Confederate Lords did not immediately suggest that Mary was concerned in the murder of her husband. It was only later that they made use of the accusation in order to depose her, and later again that they forged the Casket Letters.

The chief interest that the Casket Letters continue to hold is surely as evidence of the human, and notably the historian's, will to self-deceit. It is two hundred years since Walter Goodall by patient recourse to State Papers showed conclusively that they were forged. In his day Dr Johnson was convinced that they would never again be brought forward as evidence against Mary. Every single piece of evidence that has since come to light, and there is quite a lot, has served only to discredit them more completely.[1]

[1]It may be mentioned that the plotters destroyed all the original casket documents except one, the "marriage contract", which is still to be seen in the British Museum. It was claimed by Moray that this was the actual document "written by the Queen's awin hand, promising to marry the said Bothwell", and by Buchanan as "upon credible grounds supposit to have been made and written by hir befoir the deith of hir husband". Yet the handwriting is not hers, and

Everything to do with them smells of fraud. Mary herself was never allowed to defend herself against the accusations of the Confederate Lords when they produced the letters, of which she was not even allowed to see copies. The Regent Morton, who claimed to have discovered them, was eventually accused of being party to Darnley's murder himself, and before his execution confessed to the very crime of which he had so vehemently accused his queen. On his Danish deathbed Bothwell admitted his own guilt in the murder but denied that Mary had known anything about it. The Protestant King of Denmark sent copies of Bothwell's statement to the royal houses of Europe: Elizabeth suppressed it in England.

Yet to this day many historians cite the Casket Letters as though they were valid and acceptable documents. They carry, of course, a strong emotive appeal. To those who are determined to justify John Knox it is essential to believe that Mary was an adulteress and a murderess, for he insisted that she was. To the now more numerous section of the community who merely enjoy scandal and intrigue for their own sake the Casket Letters are equally essential, for without them Mary's story is simply the tragedy of an honest woman. And today with the strongly emotional desire to surround Elizabeth I of England with a glowing *mystique*, Mary must be maligned as much as possible in order to justify Elizabeth's despicable conduct towards her. For these reasons, and for these only, the Casket Letters are still given credence.

Although to do so upsets many of his former judgments, it is to the credit of Professor Black that in the revised (1959) edition of his volume on *The Reign of Elizabeth* in the Oxford History of England, he comes near to rejecting the Casket Letters altogether: even although one may still feel that their repeated detailed exposure, notably in Sir Edward Parry's *The Persecution of Mary*

the signature is not even a very close imitation of hers, being written with a large M such as Mary never used. Ainsworth Mitchell, the handwriting expert, has shown however in an article in *Discovery* (June, 1925), that the forming of the letters is unmistakably of the same character as the handwriting of one of her chief accusers, Maitland of Lethington. It was this piece of evidence that led Hilaire Belloc ultimately to revise his interpretation of Mary's story.

Stewart with his uncompromising demonstration that they were
"forgeries, and poor forgeries at that", rules them out of any
acceptance whatsoever. But habit dies hard amongst historians,
and Professor Black does make the effort, by no means always
made, to see Mary as a person, and to relate what we know of her
character and disposition to the character of the kind of woman
who could have entered into an adulterous connection and a plot
to murder her husband. He asks very reasonably:

> how it could come about that a woman, whose *naturel* was the
> antithesis of cruel, who was opposed to violence and bloodshed,
> who steadfastly refused to display her loyalty to the counter-
> reformation by making a holocaust of her protestant coun-
> sellors, as the papal legate, Laureo, insisted she should do: a
> woman, moreover, whose character was probably nobler than
> that of the majority of the men who surrounded her—how
> could such a one descend so suddenly, and so low, in the moral
> scale as to become an accomplice in an abominable crime, and
> so devoid of common sense, self-interest, and self-respect,
> that she gambled away not only her good name and her Scot-
> tish crown, but also her hope of the English succession, which
> had been her unalterable aim ever since she set foot on Scottish
> soil.

And he goes on to recall Elizabeth's own statement that nothing
had been "sufficiently shown" against the Queen of Scots.

In this Professor Black comes refreshingly away from a condition all too common in historians, of deciding upon facts without relation to human character and potential. Presbyterian
historians have not infrequently presented Mary as possessing
both a diabolical cunning and a profound stupidity, and a
vacillating nature and an almost superhumanly thrawn one. This
is to endeavour to create a personality out of the intellectual
residue left after making assumptions based upon preconceived
notions of events. The resultant portrait is often humanly un-
recognizable. The natural course seems to be to determine the
character of the principals in historic events from reputable contemporary documents, where these are available, making due
allowance for prejudice where it is liable to exist one way or

Mary, Queen of Scots
from the posthumous portrait at Blairs College, depicting the
execution in the background

Bishop John Geddes (1735-1799)

From the portrait at Blairs College

By permission of the Innes Review

another, and constantly to relate these personalities to the probable course of events. Catholic writers have sometimes proved themselves rather timid, a little afraid lest they might compromise their claim to judicious and lofty principle, by espousing Mary's cause too strongly. It is very largely to Protestant scholars and historians, English as well as Scots, that we owe the accumulating exposure of ancient calumny, notably to Goodall, Tytler, Hosack and Parry, but there have been many others and, as that pioneer in the practice of going to original documents as the basis of historical judgments, Agnes Strickland, demonstrated long ago, the many reliable documents relating to Mary give a very consistent picture of her character. A great many of her personal letters still exist, and her whole reign was reported upon by spies and ambassadors (often identical) to England and beyond.

Six foot tall, accounted the most beautiful princess in Europe, she was undoubtedly proud both of her position and of her person. But it was an assured pride, never petty but going together with magnanimity and a consideration for others that always gained her the devoted affection of her personal attendants, itself a revealing fact. She was charming, what psychologists sometimes describe as an anima-type, awaking quick responses in others, especially men: a characteristic often misinterpreted by the puritanical and the lecherous alike. She was exceptionally intelligent and also well educated, but, as is by no means always the case, at the same time basically a simple person; and to more complicated minds, whether those of contemporaries or of future historians, such people, those who combine quick intelligence with a directness and lack of guile, commonly prove the most baffling of all to understand.

There remains one all-important key to that understanding. This is her religion. She was throughout her life a practising Christian and Catholic. To those with no religion, who tend to believe that mankind is actuated only by emotions, inhibitions, desires, timidities and prejudices, this must make her incomprehensible. Those who have received the grace of religious faith and have had the advantage of associating with genuinely religious persons know, on the other hand, that, even with many common

F

failings, there is nothing extraordinary about a person consistently guiding her life by a clearly conceived concept of God's law and the love of Christ. Mary's religion was both informed and sincere. One of the many meaningless clichés adverted against her is that she was brought up in the "lascivious atmosphere" of the French Court. It was certainly not an inhibited atmosphere, but as far as the royal princesses were concerned it was, not unnaturally, extremely correct. Mary's regular companions were pious ladies, some of them, faced with the scandals in their own Church, much attracted to the ideas of the Reformers (one, at least, became a Protestant). She knew the arguments for and against Rome, and she had made her deliberate choice before she came home to Scotland; with one brief phase of, very understandable, uncertainty, she maintained it throughout her life, and finally gave up life itself for that faith. There is no question but that she could have saved herself had she renounced her Catholicism. Its importance in guiding her actions cannot, therefore, be over-rated.

Nor was hers a "political Catholicism". Had it been so she might have merited some of the reviling she has received from Presbyterian writers. She antagonized the Pope himself, and the leaders of the Catholic League because she would not join it, or embark upon the persecution, and even murder, that was recommended to her. Had she taken such a course it is feasible that Mary might have held her throne, and, with foreign support, kept England at bay. But the true Christian, whether Catholic or Protestant, knows that he may never practise evil in the hope that good may come of it.

The first and obvious line that men take in order to defame a woman in a position of importance is to accuse her of sexual vice. It even gives a kind of sexual satisfaction to many men to do so, while, implying that her judgment is subject to her passions, it is considered that it will totally discredit its victim. Sex was a favourite line with John Knox. He plays it so incessantly that it often makes tedious his otherwise rather crudely lively writing. His allegations against Mary's mother, Mary of Guise, are accepted as being as groundless as the long-maintained English allegations

that St Joan of Arc was a soldiers' strumpet. But he and the hired
hack, George Buchanan, have still left their mud upon Mary
Stuart.

Outside the accusations of professional and interested slanderers,
there is no contemporary evidence whatsoever that Mary was
immoral. Allegations against her virtue were never made by her
personal attendants, even when they would have been well paid
to make them. At the time when, before Darnley's death, according to Knox's later account, Mary was living in open scandal with
Bothwell, there is no reference made to any such conduct on her
part in the constant correspondence, largely inimical though it is,
sent by the ambassadors and spies about her Court. Bothwell's
seizure of her person, made with the secret support of the Confederate Lords who, he therefore knew, would never have
opposed the marriage had she been willing herself, was a forcible
abduction. Nor was this denied at the time. The Protestant James
Melville, who was captured and taken to Dunbar Castle along
with the queen, states simply, ". . . the Queen could not but marry
him seeing he had ravished her and lain with her against her will".
The Confederate Lords themselves wrote to her, urging her to
marry Bothwell for the sake of her kingdom, and she, a defence-
less widow, kept close prisoner at Dunbar with no hope of any
succour, yielded, since, in her own words written at the time: "In
a manner we are nothing, for what is a Prince without a People,
beforehand already yielded to his appetite, and as it were left
alone a Prey to him; many things we revolved with ourself but
never could find an outgait".

An account of Mary's disposition the day after the wedding
is given in the report of the French ambassador, Du Croc. She
told Du Croc, in Bothwell's presence, that "he must not be surprised if he saw her sorrowful, for she could not rejoice nor ever
would again. All she desired was death." She was in such distress
that he thought she might go mad, and she was overheard
threatening suicide when she was closeted with Bothwell.

The most cunning and basest of the plots against her, the one
aimed directly at her womanhood, was succeeding where Mary's
resource and courage had defeated so many others. Once the

wedding was over the Confederate Lords raised the cry that
Mary had murdered Darnley. Bothwell saw that he had been
outwitted. One may assume that Mary's repugnance towards him
finally destroyed his rough resolve. He escaped abroad from
Carberry Hill, and Mary, having been promised all loyalty, was
instead made prisoner, brutally handled, and, when the better
citizens of Edinburgh threatened to rescue her, hustled to the
stronghold of Lochleven Castle. A year later she escaped, only
to have her forces defeated at Langside. Trusting too well in
Elizabeth's constantly repeated promises of help and hospitality,
she crossed the border into England, and was never free again in
this world.

Certainly her faith was at its weakest at this time, for she seems
to have agreed on the strong recommendation of the Catholic
Lord Herries to "abandon the Mass" in Scotland if Elizabeth
would release and restore her to her throne. The proposal went
no further, but we should remember that Mary was still only
twenty-six, had long been prevented from practising her religion,
had undergone the most harrowing experiences, and was singularly bereft of friends and support. Shortly afterwards she consented to listen to a series of sermons by an Anglican divine, but
soon decided that there was nothing the Anglicans held that was
not better held and understood in the Church whose faithful
member she thereafter remained unto death.

For most of the nineteen years of her English imprisonment
Mary's courage was sustained by the hope that Elizabeth would
release her, or that she would be rescued or make her escape.
She never denied that she had taken part in plans to effect her
escape, nor her right to do so, nor did she deny that she had
corresponded concerning steps for her release with foreign
sovereigns, who, however, as she pointed out, were no more
foreign to her than the queen who so unjustly kept her in cap-
tivity. She always denied absolutely that she had taken any part
in plots to murder Elizabeth, and, despite desperate and elaborate
efforts, Cecil and Walsingham failed to produce the evidence that
she had so plotted. It seems unreasonable to reject Mary's own
testimony in this matter, firstly because we know her lifelong

antipathy to such methods, and secondly because we have the
evidence of her correspondence, a correspondence that reveals her
as honest and straightforward. To defend Mary is to maintain that
she was not guilty of the charges brought against her since no
available evidence of any reliability points to guilt. To defend
Elizabeth, as to defend John Knox, we have to sink our sights pretty
low, for their own written words convict them as cruel and
deceitful, liars and abettors of murder, which, unlike Mary, both
of them regarded as a legitimate political weapon. Elizabeth's
demand for more cruel methods of putting the Babington plotters
to death is characteristic of the woman whose letters trying to
arrange for Mary to be privately murdered are still in existence.
But in Mary's known letters and reliably reported statements we
find no evidence of either the cruelty or the intemperate lust that
are only imputed to her by bitter enemies and by documents
which, as Sir Edward Parry has shown, would never be admitted in
any properly constituted court of law but would have been immediately followed by prosecutions for forgery against her accusers.

Despite many deliberate and spiteful efforts by Elizabeth and
her minions to humiliate her, Mary's dignity and courage never
failed. Almost the last of the insults offered her is one worth
recalling since it clearly illustrates her final disposition. Sir Amyas
Paulet, the rough-mannered Puritan who had charge of the queen
in Fotheringhay, after she had been condemned to death ordered
that her dais and royal insignia be removed, since, in his own
courteous words, "you are a queen no longer, but already a dead
woman". At first Mary was acutely distressed by this insult to
her jealously-guarded dignity. But when, a day later, Paulet
relented and said he thought Elizabeth might allow her honours
to be restored to her, she said simply that she no longer wished
for them but had a better purpose for the space on the wall they
had occupied. She pointed to the crucifix she had hung there. She
had renounced the last of her worldly pride.

A few weeks later they brought her to the scaffold built for her
execution in the great hall of Fotheringhay. A number of eye-
witness accounts remain, all, even if reluctantly, paying tribute
to her bearing.

As the queen came towards her place of death, Melville, one of her attendants, knelt at her feet, weeping, and saying:

"Madam, it will be the sorrowfullest message that ever I carried, when I shall report that my Queen and dearest mistress is dead." Then the Queen of Scots, shedding tears, answered him, "You ought rather to rejoice than to weep, for that the end of Mary Stewart's troubles is now come. Thou knowest, Melville, that all this world is but vanity and full of troubles and sorrows: carry this message from me to my friends, that I die a true woman to my religion, and like a true Scottish woman and a true French woman. But God forgive them that have long desired my end. . . ." She passed out of the entry into the great hall, with her countenance careless, importing rather mirth than mournful cheer, so she willingly stepped up to the scaffold. . . .

Outside in the courtyard musicians played a mournful dirge, an air commonly played at the execution of witches, associating Mary's death with the same imputation laid upon Joan of Arc's. On the scaffold Dr Fletcher, Dean of Peterborough, called upon her to deny her faith. She rebuked him gently, "Mr Dean, Mr Dean, trouble me not; I am settled and persuaded in the Catholic Roman faith and mind to spend my blood in defence of it". But the Dean came close in front of her, haranguing her with great verbosity, until even the Earl of Shrewsbury was shocked at his importunity and ordered him to be silent and to begin to pray. The Dean led off with a prayer that contained a good deal of political matter, the others, except Mary's attendants, joining with him. But Mary said her own prayers, "with loud and fast voice", in Latin, repeating the *Miserere* and the *In te Domine speravi*. When the Dean had finished there was a deep silence, then Mary prayed in English:

Send me your Holy Spirit, Lord, that at the hour of my death he may enlighten me and enable me to understand the mystery of your Passion, so that I may persevere in your faith till my last breath, and that I may bear with patience the torment inflicted in my person on the Catholic Church. Grant, Lord, that my death may ensure the peace and union of all Christendom, peace between Christian princes, the conversion of England to the true faith, the perseverance of Catholics in their creed and their constancy in martyrdom. . . . As thy arms, my God, were extended on a cross, so receive me into the arms of thy mercy. Extend to me thy mercy, and pardon me all my sins. The black-masked executioners came forward to prepare their victim for the axe.

All this time [to quote at length from the official account written for Cecil] they were pulling off her apparel, she never changed her countenance, but with smiling cheer she uttered these words, that she never had such grooms to make her unready, and that she never put off her clothes before such a company. . . . This done, one of the women, having a Corpus Christi cloth lapped up three-corner-ways, kissing it, put it over the Queen of Scots' face, and pinned it fast to the caul of her head. Then the two women departed from her, she kneeling down upon the cushion most resolutely and without any token or fear of death, she spake aloud this psalm in Latin, *In te Domine confido*. Then groping for the block she laid down her head, putting her chin over the block with both hands, which holding there still, had been cut off had they not been spied. Then lying upon the block most quietly, and stretching out her arms, cried *In manus tuas, Domine*, three or four times. Then she lying very still upon the block, one of the executioners holding of her slightly with one of his hands, she endured two strokes of the other executioner his axe, she making very small noise or none at all, and not stirring any part of her from the place where she lay; and so the executioner cut off her head, saving one little gristle, which being cut in sunder, he lift up her head to the view of all the assembly, saying "God save the Queen".
It was the opinion of Benedict XIV, the Pope who in the eighteenth century established definitively the procedure of beatification, that, if only the charges connected with the names of Darnley and Bothwell could be entirely eliminated, no requisite seemed wanting for a formal declaration of Mary's martyrdom. Perhaps in time to come when Scotland sees clearly again that gaiety and clemency are of the essence of Christianity, and truth is allowed the expression that bigotry, prejudice, and the love of scandal still deny it, Mary will receive the honour that she deserves of her country.

CHAPTER IX

MARTYR

EVEN in the lifetime of John Knox the golden picture of a world liberated at last into true religion had faded: we have Knox's own agonized outcry that the bright light of revival had grown dim in a resurgent evil age, but it had never been bright as he pretended. His pride was wounded but not cast down when he found that despite the jettisoning of all that he had equated with idolatry, the new order had failed to conceive a generation of saints: he had always oversimplified the issue of good and evil, until he was little qualified to distinguish between them. In fact the establishment of the Reformed Kirk had by no means been completed by the Act of Parliament of 1560. At least half the country was Catholic, as far as it was anything, twenty-five years later. A strong Catholic leader, or a sufficiency of courageous and active priests, might well have achieved a successful counter-reform. But the Scotland of that day was tragically lacking in men of worth. The presence of a large Catholic body contributed, along with the interested opposition of the nobles, to preventing a disaster that for a time was an active threat: the imposition by the ministers of a theocratic state on the model of Calvin's Geneva. For the ministers claimed the right to absolute rule, and their activities would certainly have been condemned as seditious had the country possessed an effective civil government. Had a theocratic state been fully imposed, Scotland might have become a blood-bath: although it is not certain that the Reformed Kirk itself would have survived. As it was, for long enough under Reform Scotland merited the stricture of the Protestant historian Rowe that "a more frightful state of corruption in a Christian nation has hardly ever been recorded". The reports of the General Assembly itself deplore the increase of

"murder, oppression, adultery, incest, and all horrible crimes".
Verily, it was not the Auld Kirk that had been to blame for the
outrages of humankind.

The collapse of the secular clergy, many of whom renounced
their vows and married, while three bishops apostatized and the
rest retired in confusion, left only a few who travelled through
the country disguised as laymen trying to succour whom they
could. It was the Society of Jesus that made the first organized
attempt at regaining Scotland for the Church, and the Jesuit
became the bogey-man of the Reform. A number of the better-
educated Scots had become priests in the new Society: they
included Fr James Gordon, a cousin of the king, and Fr William
Crichton. Twice more Cecil had to move fast to prevent steps
that might have changed the future of Scotland's faith. He moved
faster than the Pope, whose two-year delay prevented Fr
Crichton's scheme for having James VI educated as a Catholic
from being carried into effect: Cecil, being informed, had the
boy king's guardian, the Duke of Lennox, sent into exile. Again,
when James had reached manhood and Fr Gordon obtained his
permission for the holding of public debates on religion and the
granting of some freedom from persecution for the Catholics,
Cecil at once sent military aid to the exiled earls of Angus and Mar,
who captured James and compelled him to sign a Protestant
alliance with England, taking over the country's government in
the alien cause.

It is perhaps necessary to observe here that Knox's Calvinism
did not make him a convinced Presbyterian. As Dr Warr puts it in
The Presbyterian Tradition:

> To regard him as the Hero of Scottish Protestantism is
> correct, but to call him the Hero of Scottish Presbyterianism
> is to assign to him a dignity which in historic fact he cannot
> claim. If his preferences lay in any direction, we are justified in
> assuming that they lay towards Episcopacy and England. Had
> England not been closed to him by Elizabeth's detestation, in
> all probability Scotland would never have seen him again
> after his desertion of its Protestant cause in 1556. Instead of
> giving his two sons to carry on his work in Scotland, he sent

them both to Cambridge to be educated for the ministry of the Anglican Church, probably anxious to fulfil in his offspring a dream which he himself had never realized.

Knox himself lived long enough to approve of the first introduction of Protestant bishops in Scotland in 1572. These were the so-called "tulchan bishops", a tulchan being a calf's skin stuffed with straw used to make a cow give its milk more freely, and were most unpopular as the creatures of the scandalous Regent Morton. It was Andrew Melville, a very much more impressive figure than Knox, a man of integrity and intellectual attainment, who effectively established Scottish Presbyterianism, getting rid of the puppet bishops and promulgating the presbyterian government of the Kirk in 1580. But uncontrolled power went to the wild heads of his little-educated colleagues. In Edinburgh they became unruly to the point of hysteria. They preached hatred and defiance, calling all kings traitors. Far more dangerous, they cried the Queen of England an atheist for her lack of Presbyterian principle. In 1596 they stirred up and led a threatening mob, and James, goaded beyond endurance, suddenly took his Court to Linlithgow and announced that he would make it his capital until the ministers recanted and Edinburgh behaved itself. The fanatical revolt collapsed like a pricked bubble, and the leading ministers fled from Edinburgh while its citizens begged the royal pardon. It is understandable that James should have retained a profound distrust of Presbyterianism. His wife, Anne of Denmark, was secretly received into the Catholic Church by a Jesuit, Fr Abercromby, in the Palace of Holyroodhouse. She tried to mollify her husband towards the Catholics, and indeed he was not unsympathetic until the skilful engineering of the Gunpowder Plot finally discredited his victims.

Thereafter the seventeenth century in Scotland sees incessant conflict in which it is not so much the Catholics who are the protagonists, although they suffered a more unremitting persecution in Scotland even than in England. The main conflict was fought out over the government of the Reformed Church: bishops versus pure Presbyterianism. It was complicated by many political issues, and later became involved with the struggle between King and Commonwealth in the sister kingdom, although there was in fact remarkably little identity of aim between the Scottish and the English Royalists or between the Covenanters and the Roundheads. The Covenanters had their own cause ever foremost, and this was no less than the spreading of Calvinist doctrine and Church government for the redemption of the whole world, starting with England. Their creed, and every other one except his own narrow faith, was anathema to Cromwell, but their blind ardour made them the ready dupes of his more astute and practical politics, while their factiousness and failure brought the fortunes of their country to the depths.

Although their cause in the fullness of its intent failed dismally, within Scotland itself the Covenanters prevailed, so that for long enough they have figured as central figures of our history. Episcopalians perhaps argue with truth that their losses and sufferings were at least as grievous, but theirs has been a minority version of history and in consequence it has not become in any similar way part of the national consciousness.

How does it seem to a Scottish Catholic? It is not for him to say with Mercutio "A pox on both your houses", even although much of the old dispute might seem largely academic to him, an internecine disagreement amongst an enemy. Episcopalians were liable to be personally more generous than Covenanters towards their Catholic neighbours, yet the only priest actually put to death during the seventeenth century was condemned under Episcopacy. But more importantly, although his faith was so long proscribed, and those who tried to practise it branded as criminals and traitors, the Scottish Catholic must see the dissentients, in whose private quarrel he had no part, not as a hiatus in the Catholic history of his country, but as still a phase in that story. Separated brethren they were, but brethren who, if in days of frenzy they condemned the faith of St Columba, yet derived all they possessed of Christianity from the Church. If human frailty vitiated their belief and action, the same frailty had brought the Church into that shameful state from which sprang their revolt. Nor can we see as merely futile the many strange byways pursued by sects and individuals. Deprived though they might be of certain channels of grace that the Catholic knows as the gifts of full membership of the visible Church, even violently denying the validity of that Church, they were still, all unconsciously, her dependants, a vital part of the wholeness of humanity that is her concern, in some manner, howsoever obscure, contributing goodwill to her growth despite the perversity of their judgment. Although most Presbyterian theology of the time is of small account, being chiefly political and polemical in nature and made particularly narrow and exclusive by the conviction that most of the world must be hell-bound, we do find such a man as Samuel Rutherford bursting through the intellectual limitations and restrictions of his creed to an apprehension of grace and a love of Christ that shines out through the rather dominant, fearful, Old Testament jargon. There is so much of the Old Testament, and it comes before the New Testament, and one may feel that the untrained mind tended to reach satiety before reaching the Gospels. Certainly the revelation of Christ often seems lost upon early Presbyterian apologists: and many at least of the martyrs of the Covenant went to their deaths with their courage fortified by a state of mind which does not seem quite to qualify them as Christian martyrs. With them it was not a case of "forgive them, Lord, for they know not what they do", but the expressed conviction that their judges were damned souls, inescapably destined to everlasting torment, men upon whose heads they could heap objurgations with all merit to themselves.

Of course the times were rough, and men had to be tough to exert their ideals at all. But in John Ogilvie, the Jesuit priest who was hanged in Glasgow in 1615, we have a man in whom the dour spirit of seventeenth-century Scotland is lit by the fuller Christian concept. In so many ways John Ogilvie is of the very essence of his time in Scotland. He was brought up a Calvinist, and a north-easterner. He was fearless and headstrong, opinionated, with just that hint of a chip on his shoulder which to this day is not uncommon amongst his people. And in the Scotland of the seventeenth century the enemy to reality was not indifferentism or a temptation to comfort and ease, but a tendency to excess, a desire for a spiritual justification for that worldly

failure which the English wars and her own corrupt statesmen
had brought upon her. In the words in which Dr Mathew opens
his valuable study, *Scotland under Charles I*: "In the seventeenth
century the climate of Scottish opinion and the organization of
Scottish social life bore little resemblance to the habits of thought
and the money-conscious stratified class system which character-
ized the southern kingdom". There was much that was admirable
about this freedom of spirit, but it was bedevilled by its concomitant narrowness, and particularly by its failure to appreciate
the warmth of the divine charity.

As a young boy John Ogilvie was sent to school abroad, for
Scottish education was not yet restored even to its status before
the breakdown of the Auld Kirk and Protestants as well as
Catholics commonly sent their sons abroad to be educated.
While still in his teens he became a Catholic, and then continued
his studies as a Jesuit. It was not until he was thirty, or a little
more, that he returned to his native Scotland.

He came then in the guise of a horse-coper, with a desire as
ardent as that of any Covenanter to win men to the faith he held.
But he came when, despite the efforts made by older Jesuits to
achieve a compromise and religious tolerance in the realm,
Catholicism was at its most oppressed. To a new generation it was
simply the Scarlet Woman, a perversion of Christian belief and
deeply involved in the machinations of foreign powers: all the
great beauty it had given to the world, the life of the Saint of
Assisi, the paintings of the primitives, the hymns of Aquinas, the
choral music—of which there seems to have been a notable
school in Scotland itself—the springtime faith of the Celtic
Church, had been lost sight of. Only the squalor of those who had
traduced the vision of the Church was adverted to and exaggerated so as to obscure her verity in a fog of scandal.

John Ogilvie, counter-reformer, *alias* Captain Watson, horse-
coper, landed at Leith in the autumn of 1613. With him came a
Capuchin priest, Fr Campbell, and another Jesuit, Fr Moffat, who
was taken at St Andrews a year later. They were like smugglers,
bringing a contraband faith, and bringing it to what we would
now call a police-state. Even when they were not the ascendant

party, the Covenanters could always worship in private how they wished, but for Catholics there was no privilege of privacy: all their prayers were penal. Their houses could at any time be broken into and search made for evidence that they worshipped in the immemorial way of Christians, which could bring down upon them fines, eviction, banishment, or death itself. The Mass was the focus of affront, by the same claim that first turned disciples away from Jesus Christ in Jerusalem: the Mass that may either be seen as the token of our redemption, or as an intolerable presumption to divine intimacy.

It was to his own part of the world, the country between Aberdeen and Banff where there were still many Catholics, that John Ogilvie took the Mass in the first autumn of his return to Scotland. Of necessity, his movements were secret, but he seems to have spent Christmas at Strathbogie, and shortly afterwards to have come south again to Edinburgh. Here he probably found it difficult at first to make contact with the Catholics, who had every reason to be suspicious for spies. Feeling, perhaps, that the odds were too heavy against them and that an alleviation of their legal status was a pre-requisite for the success of the mission, John Ogilvie made a mysterious journey to London in February 1614. Here he seems to have approached the king himself or one of his ministers, putting forward some project that might obtain greater leniency for the king's Catholic subjects and, in return, improve his standing with foreign rulers: for then, as now, the oppression of minorities always vexed international relationships. From London he crossed to Paris to report upon his scheme. But here he received a rebuff from Fr Gordon, who had seen the failure of too many such schemes in the past. Although the General of the Jesuits was more appreciative, John Ogilvie was peremptorily ordered back to his mission.

So there were to be no more politics for John Ogilvie, no more abstract efforts to improve the position of the Church in Scotland: only the relentless discomfort and suspense of a mission priest in a country where his faith was proscribed. Perhaps as he made his rather humiliating return he knew what the end must be.

He stayed in Edinburgh now, and worked alongside a Fran-

ciscan clansman of his own. There were at least three houses in
which he said Mass and exhorted his people to keep their faith
in the dead days: the homes of William Sinclair, an advocate
who was later condemned to death as a Catholic and then
banished, of Robert Wilkie and John Philipps. He made converts,
although, since he could not advertise his presence or true profession, these must have been amongst those already associated
with the Catholic community, and perhaps were rather reconciled
to a faith they had once held.

By August John Ogilvie had carried his activities to Glasgow,
where his base was the house of Marion Walker, a heroic widow
who ultimately died in prison for her religion. He reconciled
some of the Renfrewshire gentry to the faith, and began to rebuild
a Catholic congregation amongst the Glasgow merchants some
of whom were crypto-Catholics in families whose other members
knew nothing of their beliefs.

Glasgow was the See of Archbishop Spottiswoode, a Presbyterian minister who had conformed to the Episcopal Church
as it was re-established in Scotland by James VI in 1610. He was
one of the ablest and most fervent of the king's statesmen in
Scotland. A certain Adam Boyd, pretending to an interest in the
Catholic faith, had discovered the true identity of Captain Watson,
and sold his information to the Archbishop. On October 4th
at sundown Boyd arranged a meeting with the priest at the mercat
cross. James Stewart, a Protestant, although he also knew Ogilvie's
identity, tried to save him when Boyd and the archbishop's
servant came to arrest him; but he was seized and forcibly taken
to the Provost's house. Here he had his first meeting with Spottiswoode, who struck him a blow, saying, "You are overbold, Sir,
to say your Masses in a reformed city".

"You act as a hangman, Sir, and not as a bishop, in striking
me", replied John Ogilvie and was immediately violently set
upon by the mob that surrounded him.

It was not the most tactful of answers, however well merited.
But it was characteristic of John Ogilvie's still youthful impetu-
osity. Men at the approach of death are like those about to go on a
long journey. They may have appreciated for long enough that

the journey would have to be undertaken, yet at the end there is usually a rush to get packed, to jettison much that is unnecessary, finally to realize how little is essential to them now. Throughout John Ogilvie's examinations and the final trial, all of which are well documented both in his own deposition and in the reports of friend and foe, we see a kind of war with his own contempt. It is not a personal bitterness: he is not exacerbated on his own account but, like all those who are gifted with a clear and powerful intellect, he finds it difficult to be tolerant of inconsistency, hedging, and drab stupidity as shown by those bent upon his death. Although the fact that he had a quicker wit and, with the long schooling of the Society of Jesus behind him, a far better trained mind than his judges, enabled him to make a devastating case against them, it also made it more difficult for him to be patient.

The Scottish bishops who examined him were in a weak position, as Ogilvie reminded them when he said, "This religion you talk about is not ten years old yet; when I was a boy you believed there was no head of the Church save Christ alone, and you forbade men to say otherwise. Now you all take oath and subscribe to the doctrine that the King is head of the Church in his own kingdom. You used to take oath and subscribe to the denial of that doctrine. . . . That cannot be Apostolic teaching for Paul says: 'If I destroy what I have built up I make myself a liar . . .'." Then, turning to Andrew Knox, Bishop of the Isles: "You used to preach at Paisley against episcopacy; yes, you said 'if anyone is made a bishop, I shall openly call him a devil and say that he deserves to be spat upon!' A fortnight after that you were made a bishop. And you were not content with the bishopric of the Isles, but took a fatter one in Ireland as well. Yes, and William Andrew Couper wrote a book against the order of bishops: he is Bishop of Galloway today."

Ogilvie, like the Covenanters, stood for the supremacy of the Church in things spiritual. Like theirs, his stand was a very old one, a defence of essential human liberty against a tyranny intrinsically the same as that we have come to experience in our own day under dictatorship and Communism. Unlike the

Covenanters, he had behind him the wisdom and charity of the Universal Church. The doctrinaire Covenanter believed that in the event of misrule in the opinion of the people, or a section of the people, or even in the private judgment of an individual, a king might justly be assassinated. As such, their persecution by the king was at least understandable. Ogilvie recognized the temporal rights of his king, and condemned assassination outright. Furthermore, he saw his judges as possessed of immortal souls which, even although they might be jeopardizing them, were as open to salvation as his own. As a Christian he could not bolster his courage with the hatred that rejoiced to see in them damned children of Satan, predestined for hell.

The Catholic Church has frequently been miscalled "reactionary" in the sense of opposing principles of human liberty, although in this context the word is meaningless since it presupposes such liberty the prerogative of "progress", whereas we have seen all too often a "progress" that is the very antithesis of liberty. Liberty is always under threat from human aggrandizement. John Ogilvie stands a champion of liberty, not of an anarchy denying the rights of a civil government, but upholding the individual's essential freedom under that régime. For the State that tried him it must be said, however, that he was given a public trial, whatever its shortcomings in its efforts to condemn him for treason and not merely for being a priest. An open trial is always some concession to justice. Although at first the spreading of the rumour that he had betrayed his fellow Catholics caused him to be execrated, when it was realized that even under torture he had betrayed no one he gained public sympathy, both Catholic and Protestant.

He was taken to Edinburgh to the Tolbooth where he was subjected to the torture that was considered most likely to extort confession and betrayal, a more primitive version of modern methods of brainwashing. He was forcibly kept awake for nine nights and eight days, with blows and noises, needles driven under his nails and the pulling out of his hair. The torture was only discontinued when he was in imminent danger of death. Although he had been reduced to a state in which, on his own testament, he

G

hardly knew if and what he spoke, he gave nothing away. After being allowed a day and a night of rest he was brought into the judgment hall and threatened with worse tortures. He replied: "Had I been willing to answer your questions before, I would not do so now, lest I should appear to obey like a beast to blows, when I would not be led by argument. Do your worst; I will give you as many bones to break as you have instruments of torture; I was born for things above sense, and I trust not in myself but in God's grace. What you do, do quickly; it is all I ask."

Three months later John Ogilvie was given a formal trial in Glasgow before being taken out to the gallows already prepared for him. During part of that time he had been treated well while efforts were made to bribe him to renounce his faith. But most of it he had spent chained and shackled. To him it was a time of intensive preparation, a curbing of such contempt and intolerance as he might feel for his accusers, constant prayer for the grace to die in charity for all men. When he was able to make contact with his friends, it was for their prayers that he asked, prayers that he might be given strength and perseverance to the end: for he knew that he could not do what he had to do by himself, he had renounced that vainglory.

They hanged him in Glasgow on the last day of February, 1615. A minister, Robert Scot, humane and presumptuous, first begged him to recant and accept the life and position offered him, then, when he refused, called to the crowd that his execution was not for any question of faith but for treason to the king. John Ogilvie protested at this falsehood, and made it clear that he died for his faith alone, and so died willingly. He embraced his executioner, forgiving him. The executioner said, "Say, John, 'Lord have mercy on me. Lord receive my soul' ". John Ogilvie repeated the prayer offered him in such strange friendship. He was swung off the ladder. Out of respect, his executioner instead of jumping on his shoulders pulled at his feet to put him out of his last suffering.

From the scaffold John Ogilvie had flung his rosary into the watching crowd. It struck a young Hungarian Calvinist, Jean de Eckersdorff, who had come to see the show. It was a blow of faith, and the young man became John Ogilvie's last convert. Three centuries later an artist from Hungary made the statue of the martyr that stands in the church of the Society of Jesus in Edinburgh.

CHAPTER X

MISSION PRIESTS

CROSSES and shrines had been smashed and desecrated. Only the holy wells could not be removed: their clear water still bubbled up from the earth, and, in spite of fulminations from the pulpits, generations of Protestants otherwise correct took their secret wishes to the wells named after long-forgotten saints. In its enthusiasm for "pure" religion the Kirk had tried to secularize human life; theirs the heresy of the Manicheans, the idea that the world that God made is itself evil, no better than a tangle of temptations to the pilgrim soul. Where the old faith had tried to hallow the things of the world, nature and art alike, the new faith in Scotland sought to ostracize them, seeing itself the Democracy of Saints, and in its enthusiasm never apprehending that it is only the heroic few whose spirituality has the sheer buoyancy to transcend the common life and then only after a growth made arduously through love, not assumed in contempt.

To criticize the words and deeds of the early preachers is in no way to belittle the real piety of the lives of countless Presbyterians through the ensuing centuries. It is only to make an effort to dispel a legend long propagated: the idea that the Scottish Reformation saw the triumph of reason and a purified religion. If we go to contemporary documents it is depressing to find how small a part reason did play in the equipment of the first leaders of Presbyterianism. They themselves were not altogether ignorant of their ignorance, and from John Knox onwards were reluctant to be drawn into public debate with Catholics, and, if challenged, usually replied by appeal to the penal laws in order to have their opponents imprisoned or banished. Their spoken and written controversy took the form almost entirely of tedious diatribe depending upon crude sexual analogy to whip up a prurient revulsion against the old faith: "the mother of harlots, and so old indeed, but old in adulteries and who because of her whoredoms is the mistress of witchcrafts, whose skirts the Lord has discovered upon her face, and will more and more show the nations her nakedness, and the kingdoms her shame, who at last shall hate the whore, make her desolate, eat her flesh, and burn her with fire, for strong is the Lord who judgeth her . . ." to quote a characteristic passage from Dr William Guild of Aberdeen, reckoned one of the most distinguished Presbyterian polemicists of the seventeenth century.

Dr Johnson was amused at the ignorance of the Papist who declared that the Lord's Prayer was a good prayer and he wondered who had written it. The Presbyterian preachers knew who had composed the Lord's Prayer but they did not think it was a very good one. Information about God might be more widespread but men's knowing of God had declined as doctrine had narrowed, gaining fervour without spiritual depth. Dr Pitcairn records one minister, late in the seventeenth century, who after analysing the Lord's Prayer and showing how inferior it was to the long extempore prayers with which the ministers "wrestled" in the kirk, decided that our Lord must have been drunk when he composed it. This loss of a sense of the supernatural, to say nothing of a sense of humour, in favour of the public expression of private judgment was part of an intellectual fallacy sustained by men whose mental attainments were usually slight. Actually this rejection of the saying of the Lord's Prayer and the Apostles' Creed in church was not part of the origins of Scottish Presbyterianism, but was introduced, oddly enough, from England during the Puritan ascendancy and the short-lived marriage of the two countries' Churches that produced the Westminster Confession with its strange and depressing doctrine. It was a doctrine from which the English quickly wriggled free but left as the official dogma of the Church of Scotland, a patchwork compromise born of political expediency between two mutually hostile establishments. Thus for no willing reason the Lord's Prayer long remained in discredit, and even at the end of the eighteenth century a minister gave grave offence by using it at the opening of the Law Courts instead of indulging a demonstration of original talent.

The superstition of Calvin made his churches particularly guilty in the orgies of witch-hunting and burning that are such a blot on the sixteenth and seventeenth centuries. In earlier mediaeval times there was none of it: in fact, belief in witchcraft was considered unchristian. It is interesting that witch-hunting was introduced under the influence of those Renaissance ideas that are supposed to have been entirely enlightening, and it was first given encouragement by a Papal Bull of 1484. The Spanish Inquisition, for all its savagery with intellectual heretics, refused to accept allegations of witchcraft, so that Spain remained an honourable exception to the witch-hunt that brought terror, torture and death to hundreds of thousands of persons, chiefly women, most of whom were innocent of any crime. Although James VI wrote a celebrated book on witchcraft, as he grew older, discovering for himself the appalling abuse and victimization to which witch-hunting led, he discountenanced his former policy. Charles I lost a good deal of support amongst the common people because the Royalists would not witch-hunt, and Cromwell gained support by his favourable attitude to a pursuit which was popular amongst the uneducated particularly where puritanism had suppressed more innocuous outlets. In Scotland there was little witch-hunting until after the Reformers passed a savage and stupid Act in 1563, which stimulated superstitious fears that, from the records, seem to have been always at their worst when the Presbyterian party was dominant. Dr Black, in his study of the subject, suggests 1590-97, 1640-44, and 1660-63 as the worst periods of persecution in Scotland.[1] An English traveller records

[1]To convey something of the evil effects of witch-hunting it is enough to quote the account of an interview with a condemned "witch" given by Sir George Mackenzie, the celebrated seventeenth-century judge, not himself much opposed to the practice. "I went when I was a Justice-depute to examine some women, who had confest judicially, and one of them, who was a silly creature, told me under secresie that she had not confest because she was guilty, but being a poor creature, who wrought for her meat and being defam'd for a witch, she knew she would starve, for no person thereafter would either give

seeing nine witches burnt at one time on Leith Links. In Scotland
at least the victims were nearly always strangled before being
burnt, but torture was regularly used to extort "confessions". In
the seventeenth century one witch-finder, who was eventually
exposed and hanged, admitted to having had over two hundred
and twenty witches burnt in Scotland and the North of England,
for which he received a pound a time. The last witch-burning
took place in Scotland at Dornoch in the year 1727, and the relevant statutes were repealed ten years later, to the great indignation
of the Presbyterian Secession which was still complaining against
a repeal "contrary to the express law of God" fifty years afterwards.

But the Scottish Inquisition maintained by the Kirk Sessions
did not limit itself to suspected heretics and witches but was much
concerned with carnal transgressions, for which men and women
could be hanged. Excommunication by the Kirk meant outlawry.
Only very slowly was power taken from the Kirk Sessions and
put under the less hysterical care of the civil authority.

Of course puritanism is a common outcome of oppression in
Catholic countries as well as in Protestant. Grim years of history,
an enforced narrowing of the national horizon, the straitening of
poverty, all threatened Scotland with a demoralization that could
only be countered by some toughening of the nation's character.
Doubtless it led to much that was narrow and ugly, but, while it
serves no good to deny this strand in our past, it would be equally
foolish to blind ourselves to the virtues that developed despite the
constrictions of a Calvinism that gradually became modified and
mollified. Nor is there any sense in regarding this process as one
of emancipation achieved from intolerable restriction merely by
"natural man". Our Calvinist forebears might be intellectually
confused, but they shared the heritage of baptism and access to
graces that, even if their dialectic denied their existence, are plainly
manifest in the lives of generations of Scottish people. However
sternly doctrine and dogma reverted to the Old Testament and,

her meat or lodging, and that all men would beat her, and hound Dogs at her,
therefore she desired to be out of the World; whereupon she wept bitterly, and
upon her knees called God to witness to what she said."

in Calvinist predestination, promulgated a creed that could not be equated with the Christian concept of redemption, rays of light were always breaking through from the New Testament, for there are merciful gaps between the thickest bars of the iron defensive cage that man makes of his ideas.

Although since the days of the Celtic saints the Church has always been embodied in some part of the people of Scotland, her original organization came to an end with the death of the last of the Catholic bishops in the fateful year, 1603, that took the king to London. Archbishop James Beaton had fled the country in 1560. He still served Scotland as ambassador during his exile in Paris and was held in such esteem by the king that in 1598 he ordered the Scots Parliament to restore all his honours and emoluments despite his religion. It may be mentioned that King James held a like respect for the exiled Bishop of Dunblane, who ended his life a Carthusian monk, and actually tried to have him raised to the cardinalate—an effort blocked by the vigilant Cecil. One other of the old bishops, John Leslie of Ross, who after imprisonment in England went to France and became Vicar-General of Rouen, deserves to be remembered for his valuable *History of Scotland*.

There were left in the country perhaps half a dozen secular priests. In 1599 they had been put under the jurisdiction of the arch-priest of England, a move they much resented. There was good reason for their disliking it, for the English were always ignorant of the situation in Scotland, as, indeed, they themselves appreciated, so that both parties petitioned for an independent Scottish mission, although half a century was to pass before the secular priests of Scotland were granted their own Prefect-Apostolic. This lack of co-ordination and leadership placed them at a great disadvantage.

The Regular clergy were better placed, being provided with direction and modest funds by their own superiors. Besides the Jesuits there were a few Benedictines and Franciscans. Then, about 1620, Irish missionaries came once again to the Highlands and Islands. The first of these were Franciscans. They came to island communities some of whom had not even heard of the Reforma-

tion, for the Presbyterians had largely overlooked their existence
and those ministers who came were little liked. Priests were
received with a touching devotion, and the people flocked to
them for instruction. In Rome Propaganda could hardly believe
that one Franciscan had converted or reconciled 10,269 persons
to the Church. Indeed, Propaganda showed a tragic inability to
grasp the need and readiness of the Gaelic-speaking Highlanders
for missionaries. The mission was always undermanned and inadequately financed. The priests worked under almost incredible
conditions of poverty and privation, often thankful if they got
as much as one meal a day, of oatcake and cheese. One of them, a
Scottish Capuchin, Fr Lindsay, went about his labours disguised
as a shepherd, playing the bagpipes at fairs and gatherings where
he might discover Catholics. He was three times betrayed, but
always escaped. He must have been a man of amazing vigour, for
he lived to be eighty-four, dying in the utter poverty counselled
for his sons by St Francis of Assisi.

Lack of support from Rome and the capture of their priests
in Scotland brought an end to the work of the Franciscans for the
time being. But after an appeal for priests sent from South Uist
by MacDonald of Clanranald, Propaganda approached St Vincent
de Paul and asked if he would send some of his Congregation to
Scotland. It is pleasant to be able to recall that that most lovable
and heroic of saints, despite his enormous commitments, which
included the reconversion of parts of France devastated and even
reduced to cannibalism in wars that were largely promoted by
cynical Princes of the Church, sent three missionaries to Scotland.
All were men fired with his own zeal. Fr Lumsden, a Scot, came
to the northern Highlands and to Orkney. Two Irish priests, Fr
Duggan and Fr White, came to the Hebrides, where they consolidated the people in the faith from Barra to Benbecula. After
five years Fr Duggan was about to extend his mission north to
Harris and Lewis when he took ill and died.

The Hebridean mission was next put under the Archbishop of
Armagh, Blessed Oliver Plunkett. There had, of course, been no
confirmations in Scotland since the bishops left. Blessed Oliver
Plunkett planned to visit the Isles in person, dressed in a kilt. His

martyrdom at Tyburn prevented his ever making the visit. He and others strongly recommended the training of native Highland priests, but liaison with Rome remained bad and the scheme was constantly shelved. We have records of only two native Gaelic-speakers being ordained at this time, Fr Aeneas MacDonald of Glenaladale and Fr Robert Munro. Fr Alexander Leslie, who made a visitation in 1679 when Fr Munro and three Irish priests were at work in the Highlands, wrote of the Island of Barra in a letter to Propaganda:

I visited every district, and the Sacraments were administered and all the services held for the benefit of the Catholics, who gathered round us every day with equal joy to them and to us. When we were on the point of leaving the inhabitants showed themselves much displeased with Munro because he would not remain with them, and if I had not been with him I firmly believe that they would have kept him by force. Indeed they had some idea of keeping me, imagining that as I was an official of the Pope, if they detained me in their power they could make a treaty with His Holiness to obtain priests from him as a ransom for his delegate. I had as much as I could do, even backed by the laird, to escape from them, and then only by promising to go to Rome and throw myself at the feet of His Holiness and put before him their neglected condition and their spiritual needs. At length after much weeping and many laments they agreed that I should depart, and Munro with me, but they swore blood-curdling oaths that if they did not get a priest of their own and Munro or any other came to the island, he would not be allowed to leave except by swimming, as he would get no boat. They swore that they would sooner burn their boats than let another priest leave in one. Indeed, it would be quite in keeping with the character of these islanders that they would send an expedition to steal the priest of a neighbouring locality, and this would be the cause of deadly enmity between them.

Fr Munro worked for thirty-four years on the mission. Several times he was imprisoned and twice banished. Although his subsequent returning qualified him for the death penalty, the shrewd decision not to make any more martyrs of Catholic priests pre-

served his life. Yet his death in 1704 when, an old man and
suffering from a high fever, he was thrown into a dungeon of
Glengarry Castle by the English garrison, without straw
to lie on or water to drink, seems martyrdom indeed.

In 1644 Mgr Rinuccini, an Italian bishop, published his book,
Il Cappucino Scozzese, which has been described by M. V. Hay
as either "a late example of mediaeval hagiography or an early
specimen of the historical novel". It was a romantic story of a
priest on the Scottish mission and became very popular in France
as well as in Italy. But its vivid inaccuracies made it a source of
added exasperation to the Scottish priests. There was little enough
romance in their lives, but danger, poverty, squalid living conditions and constant disappointment. If those on the Lowland
mission might at times receive the comfort of hospitality in the
few noble houses that maintained the faith and which provided
the best centres for their work, they never had the comparative
safety afforded by the more solidly Catholic communities of the
Isles and certain secluded pockets of the mainland. They lived
under constant threat to themselves and to all who befriended
them from the vigilant ministry and its supporting soldiery.
Lack of organization and therefore of leadership made for further
frustration which found an unfortunate outcome in disagreements
between Jesuits and secular priests, a running quarrel that long
handicapped their cause. The lot of the secular priest was particularly hard. Whereas the Regulars if they had to retire through
age or ill-health had their Continental houses to receive them,
there was no such provision for the secular priests. Their health
was often ruined while they were still young by undernourish-
ment, sleeping in the open, and the imprisonment and violence
they received. At home or abroad they could look for no certain
succour, and many of them died in extreme want.

To those with no religion, of course, the exertions of these
priests can only seem pathetic and wasteful of talents, and they
were usually men of more than common ability. The cause they
espoused was one that, throughout most of Scotland, can hardly
be said to have prevailed. Their work, their self-sacrifice and the
patriotism that brought them back to Scotland to a life hidden,

poor and dangerous, have received little or no commemoration in the standard histories of our country: rather they, the Jesuits in particular, have been stigmatized as traitors—traitors for sustaining the faith of Ninian and Columba who founded this country in Christianity. To them it was enough if they could bring the Mass and the doctrine of the Church to some amongst their own countrymen. And to all to whom Christianity is primarily what it claims to be, not a social service nor to be justified by any future success in the world, but the means of each individual man's most immediate access to God through his Redeemer, their work was justified and triumphant.

CHAPTER XI

NEW BISHOPS

I N 1653 William Ballantyne was appointed Prefect-Apostolic of the Scottish mission. Although his powers did not extend far, they did enable him to make a beginning in co-ordinating the work of the secular priests. Fr Ballantyne was a minister's son, probably born in North Berwick, an able scholar and a man of charm and stately good looks which made a reassuring impression upon some of the Protestants. Unfortunately he was taken prisoner on a journey through England and had to spend three years of confinement in London, and then linger in Paris until he could get the money to pay his prison debts, only returning to Scotland a year before his death in 1661. He was buried in the Huntly vault in the ruins of Elgin Cathedral, and—a breath of kindliness—a number of Protestants, including the magistrates of the town, came to his funeral.

William Ballantyne was succeeded by Alexander Winster, a native of Moray. During Winster's Prefectship Fr Alexander Leslie made his visitation on behalf of Propaganda, spending four years gathering material for his report which was completed in 1681. At this time, when the population of Scotland was perhaps more than half a million, he reckoned there were hardly fifteen thousand Catholics left. Of these, twelve thousand were in the Highlands and Islands: of Lowland counties Banffshire had the highest number, about a thousand, and Galloway the next with a little over half as many; Aberdeenshire came next again. The report once more makes earnest recommendation that a bishop should be appointed. But before that was done there came sharp changes in the status of Catholics in Scotland, very briefly a change for the better, then darkness again. Religious toleration came under James VII in 1687 with complete freedom of worship for Catholic and Covenanter alike. Jesuits were brought to

Holyrood to run a school and a printing press. The ancient abbey church was restored and finely decorated. But in 1688 Revolution followed. Holyrood once again suffered destruction at the hands of the rabble mob. Priests were hunted and imprisoned. Fr Burnet escaped from Edinburgh to Speyside where he and Fr Alexander Leslie spent a month on the moors without any shelter, and the whole winter from November to March in a little hut built of loose stones, often buried beneath snow. The final triumph of Presbyterianism followed, and Episcopalians became more friendly with Catholics a little of whose persecution they now shared until the Union of 1707.

As is now known, King William III was himself mainly responsible for the massacre of the Episcopalian MacDonalds of Glencoe in 1692, an ugly piece of intimidation by government of a kind that is more common in the English than in the Scottish past. But even here an element of the family feuds that play a much larger part in Scottish history obtruded, and the MacDonalds' old enemies, the Campbells, were much involved. It may be remarked that the clannishness and family regard that marks Scottish life was able at times to bridge even the gulf of religious division, and Catholics might on occasion receive protection from their Protestant clansmen.

The last supporters of James VII, many of them Catholics, held the impregnable rock fortress of the Bass in the Firth of Forth from 1691 to 1694. Priests came in a ship from Dunkirk to serve them, and were taken prisoner when finally the garrison had to surrender.

While on the surface the Catholic cause might seem at a low ebb at the close of the seventeenth century, the devotion of the priests and the consolidation of a laity, many of whom had perhaps come to see more clearly and certainly that what they sought to sustain was of irreplaceable value, had effected a deeper change. This retrenchment was manifested by the appointment at last, in the dark days of 1695, of Thomas Nicolson as Scotland's first Vicar-Apostolic, and, in spite of continued persecution, in less than a hundred years after Fr Leslie's census, the number of Catholics doubled.

Thomas Nicolson was born about the year 1642 in the charming little house of Birkenbog that still stands in the Banffshire countryside. He was of good family and intelligence, and studied at Aberdeen University, becoming a professor in Glasgow before he was thirty. In 1682 he resigned his professorship on being received into the Catholic Church. Now he followed so many of his countrymen into exile on the Continent. It is of interest that this Catholic exodus should have a lasting memorial in the Royal Scots, who, after years of foreign service, were brought home by Charles I and established as the oldest regiment and the first of the line in the British Army. "The Father of the Regiment", Sir John Hepburn, was a Catholic, as were his successor, Lord James Douglas, and the majority of their men.

From Douai Thomas Nicolson went to a University post in Padua where he was ordained priest in 1686. But his exile was only a temporary one, and he returned to France to prepare himself for the Scottish mission. For about a year he worked in the Glasgow district, but was arrested during the Revolution and spent several months in prison in Edinburgh before being banished and going, a sick man, to Dunkirk where he became chaplain to the English nuns.

In 1694 Nicolson's was one of six names put forward by Fr William Leslie to the Cardinal Protector in Rome, since, as Fr Leslie wrote, "after 40 years work and incredible difficulties, it has pleased God Almighty to inspire the Pope, his Vicar upon Earth, to grant a Bishop to Scotland; yea, and to maintain him of the monies of the Propaganda, besides what is already allowed to the missionaries".

This missionary bishopric was quite a different proposition to the benefices which had been the source of such interested jockeying in pre-Reformation days. Utterly impoverished, the Church in Scotland was no longer carrion for great families, a chief means to wealth, power and advancement. Purged of luxury, her marks were once again poverty and humility. She had come back the hard way to her origins. Thomas Nicolson had already shown his disposition when he had exchanged his agreeable life as a Glasgow professor for the uncertainty, discomfort and ostracism of a Catholic priest in penal times. The bishopric he was offered was no sinecure, although, feeling himself inadequate for the difficulties it presented, he at first refused it, but was eventually persuaded, and consecrated in secret in the chapel of the Archbishop of Paris.

In the event it is doubtful if a better choice could have been made for the first Scottish prelate of the new order. It was two years, which included a sojourn in an English prison, before Bishop Nicolson was able to make his way by stealth into Scotland. He went to his own Banffshire countryside, to the secluded house at Preshome that was long to remain the home of the Vicars-Apostolic. From here in the autumn of 1697 he sent his first report in which he is able to testify to the excellence of the few missionaries still at work, but deplores a wretched state of ignorance and immorality in the country as a whole. In 1700 he made a visitation to the Hebrides. He had then, and generally thereafter, to travel by remote tracks to avoid the English soldiers. He came to Moidart and the Rough Bounds, poor but beautiful with their mountains and deep-cutting sea lochs, in their isolation strongholds of the faith. He sailed from the harbourage of Arisaig to the Island of Eigg with its great Sgurr of basalt, and there found three hundred Catholics "very constant in the faith". He sailed on to the sea-divided Island of Canna, where there were one hundred and thirty Catholics to welcome him. He crossed the rough waters of the Minch, bringing confirmation to the fifteen hundred Catholics of South Uist. He visited Benbecula and Barra, before returning by Morar, going up the coast to secluded Knoydart, and inland again by Glengarry and the Great Glen. He stationed no less than ten missionaries, seculars, Franciscans and a Benedictine, and drew up his *Statuta Missionis* which regulated the work of the mission for eighty years. The Jesuits were still centred on the houses of Lowland nobles, but the following year they made formal and complete submission to the bishop's authority, and thereafter they too served in the Highland area.

Although he always resolutely refused to mix himself in politics, having more important work to do, Bishop Nicolson had another spell of imprisonment when he was over seventy after the failure of the Rising of 1715. Three years later he died at Preshome, having kept the faith and fought a good fight with weapons of peace. He is buried along with thirty other mission priests in the graveyard appropriately dedicated to St Ninian in the Enzie.

Thomas Nicolson with his resolution, courage and charity, is a better hero for his countrymen than so many of those who figure with such grandiosity in our history books, men who might be sincere but whose factiousness and narrowness do us little credit and served to waste much of the good they might have done for their country. Presbyterians long remained too pro-testant in the negative sense, witch-hunting for Catholics, more concerned to suppress papistry, with violence if need be, than to set their own house in order and win men to loyalty by the example of wisdom: prison and banishment and the crying of scandal were their too-ready arguments. Bishop Nicolson's labours called forth only fury from the more vocal of the ministers, the violence of whose rather unlettered prejudice seemed to blind them to the work of charity.

Although Bishop Nicolson did much to heal the internal strife of the Catholic mission as it existed between Jesuit and secular priest, the trouble broke out again and continued intermittently for many years, doing harm to a cause that was precarious enough already. It was rooted in the allegations of Jansenism in those seculars who had been trained at the Scots College at Paris, made by the Jesuits who had always been fervent in their opposition to the heresy and were quick to suspect its influence. Although it does not seem that Jansen's condemned beliefs were ever actually held in the Scottish mission, their austere implications certainly exerted an influence in both teaching and practice. It was prob-ably inevitable, for three reasons. Firstly, many of the mission priests were trained in France, whose Church was for a time much tainted with Jansenism. Secondly, the Calvinist background against which they worked in Scotland lent its kindred colour to their religion. Thirdly, the austerities forced upon them by the penal laws naturally emphasized the concept of immolation

H

in their creed, and tended to make rigorists of them.

Bishop Nicolson's successor, James Gordon, a man of like calibre, suffered from time to time in his long episcopacy from reckless allegations that he was a Jansenist: his reputation was firmly cleared when on his death Pope Benedict XIV paid a fine tribute to his work on the Scottish mission, describing him as "one of the greatest bishops of the Christian world". In the eighty-one years of his life Bishop Gordon had to labour in the face of many heavy reverses, although he died a few weeks before the disaster of Culloden was to bring a new and more bloody persecution by the English troops and their German allies.

Also a Banffshire man, James Gordon studied at Douai, worked on the Scottish mission, and then, at the age of forty, while in Rome, was appointed coadjutor-bishop. From 1706 he was able to take over some of his arduous episcopal journeys from Bishop Nicolson. After Bishop Gordon's first visitation to the West, during which he confirmed 2,242 persons, he conducted the first ordination in Scotland since the Reformation, raising to the priesthood Fr Dalglish at Scotshouse in Knoydart. A bad phase of persecution following, Bishop Gordon went himself to Edinburgh to try to have some influence brought to bear upon the London Government which had newly absorbed the old Scottish Parliament. From Edinburgh he sent Fr Carnegie to London, where the intervention of foreign ambassadors gained a mitigation that lasted until 1715.

It was during this time that Bishop Gordon founded a seminary on an island in the beautiful setting of Loch Morar. Thereafter the West Highland seminary occupied various sites, including Samalaman and the Isle of Lismore. In 1714 a second seminary was opened at Scalan, on the site of the simple little college building that still stands: there it had a dozen students by 1726, when Bishop Gordon had to disperse them because of ministerial enmity. The following year Scotland was divided into two Vicariates, Highland and Lowland, although it was not until 1731 that the first Vicar-Apostolic of the Highland District was appointed. Bishop Hugh MacDonald had been one of the two first "heather priests"—those educated entirely in penal Scotland, ordained just before the closing of the seminary at Scalan. He was a son of the Laird of Morar and he reopened the seminary on its island, "the most proper place in all this nation where by boat all necessities can be brought, and all unnecessary distractions kept off".

In the summer of 1745 Bishop MacDonald learnt of the arrival of Prince Charles Edward. He felt the time was not propitious, and went quickly to Arisaig, boarding the French man-of-war where he himself, as was usual, disguised as a layman, he spoke with the Prince who was disguised as a priest! When the Prince refused to take his advice to return to France, Bishop MacDonald came with him to Glenfinnan, blessed the royal standard and appointed some of his priests to act as chaplains to the Jacobite army.

Although by no means the majority of those who joined the Prince's army, Catholics naturally came in force to fight for a change to the régime that oppressed them so harshly. The Jacobite army deserves lasting honour and respect for the humanity it showed throughout its campaign both in Scotland and in England. Unfortunately the Hanoverian troops were quite a different body, their conduct shameful even by modern standards of savagery. After Culloden, Cumberland loosed his troops upon the Highland people in a campaign of murder, rape, and burnings, and many were sent as slave labour to the colonies. The Catholics, whether or not they had been out with the Prince, were chief victims of this cult of horror. The penal laws were tightened: orders given that all priests were to be arrested and all chapels demolished. The seminary at Scalan was plundered and burnt. Many priests were imprisoned and banished, two Jesuits dying in prison. Some of the island lairds, Clanranald, MacNeil of Barra and MacDonald of Boisdale, whose families had kept the faith, now apostatized. Boisdale began a bitter persecution of his people in South Uist, which they met with extraordinary bravery. He later changed in his attitude, and died calling for a priest, a mercy his sons denied him.

Yet at the same time, equally in character, during this time of intensified persecution when no worldly advantage lay with it, there were many conversions to the faith. The converts were a varied lot, fulfilling the Church's role as home of both sinner and saint. The old Lord Lovat, whose long life of self-indulgence and double-dealing was soon to come to an end on a London scaffold, received the grace of conversion, or perhaps reconciliation, at the ministration of Bishop Hugh MacDonald himself. This was on the seminary island of Loch Morar where Lovat and the bishop and the bishop's brother had gone into hiding. Another convert was Alasdair MacMaighstir Alasdair, one of the greatest of Gaelic poets, and compiler of the first dictionary of his language: a stormy, poetic character and inveterate Jacobite. Very different was the young medical student, George Hay, who, a boy of sixteen, had accompanied the Prince's army as a non-combatant, attending the wounded of both sides, but none the less was sent prisoner to London, and whose conversion gave Scotland another of her great bishops of penal days.

Bishop Hugh MacDonald succeeded in escaping and reaching France. Three years later he returned to Scotland and went to live at Shenval in the Cabrach. The representations of foreign ambassadors had once again shamed the Government into mitigating the Scottish persecution, but eventually Bishop Mac-Donald was arrested. Now, however, a kinder spirit was allowed play and he was released on the legal quibble that he was a bishop and the wording of the act only referred to priests! He returned to the north, and died in 1773 at Aberchalder near Fort Augustus, "an old man, much broken down by the fatigues of his office, and the hardships of those disturbed times".

By then George Hay had been appointed Bishop of the Low-land half of Scotland. His conversion is interesting in its pattern of a return to the faith of a member of a family that had been zealous in support of John Knox. Latterly they had favoured episcopacy. To the evangelical piety of his mother, moreover, Bishop Hay always paid devoted tribute, seeing it less as the expression of heresy than as the matrix of his own return to the fullness of Catholic faith. An austere man, at the other end of his long life he was in his turn to make a favourable impression upon Presbyterians, and to help to allay the almost paranoiac fear and superstition that had been inculcated in Scotland and used to hedge in the members of its Kirk from looking beyond the limits of their own dogma. He himself had, in the usual way, been convinced that Catholicism was totally opposed to Christianity, until he first met some Catholics in the Prince's army, and later in prison in London. On his release he retired for a time to the country to avoid being called as witness against his fellow Jacobites. Here he began to learn more of Catholic doctrine through reading and prayer, and entered a period of terrible misgiving. Back in Edinburgh he became on sufficiently friendly terms with his fencing master, John Gordon of Braes, to ask him if he knew of any Catholics whom he might meet. John Gordon then confided that he was himself a Catholic. Fr John Seton, s.j., was the priest in Edinburgh at the time and he instructed and received the young man.

George Hay was studying medicine under the famous Dr John Rutherford at the Royal Infirmary. He was one of Rutherford's best pupils, and remained a lifelong friend of his master, but, of course, as a Catholic he was not allowed to graduate or set up as a doctor in Scotland. The best he could do was to sign on as a ship's surgeon, a post for which qualifications were then regarded somewhat casually. It was while on his way to join his ship in London that he visited Bishop Challoner, who first encouraged him to find his vocation in the priesthood, and in whom he gained an even more intimate friend. He studied at the Scots College in Rome and was ordained in 1759. In 1769 he was made coadjutor to Bishop Grant, third Vicar-Apostolic of the Lowland District, whom he duly succeeded ten years later.

The forty-two years of George Hay's bishopric really saw the emergence of the Church in Scotland from the catacombs to which it had been consigned for so long. It was neither a steady nor an easy process, but it persisted. Bishop Hay was to come to find himself sympathetically received when he asked for leases and for materials for building "Mass-houses" from Protestants: and once was even greeted with the remark, "As for the better religion, that won't be known till the Day of Judgment!" This seems a logical attitude, consistent with private judgment, and a liberation from the superstitious dread that had long bedevilled the Presbyterian attitude to the Auld Kirk. A Catholic could not quite reciprocate in the same terms, but still, the Catholic attitude had also undergone wholesome change. The over-simple notion, widely held, that all who were in heresy were necessarily also in bad faith was giving place to a clearer apprehension of the mystery of faith. This greater understanding not only improved the Catholic's relationship with his Protestant neighbours but, like a kind of spiritual emancipation, also gave him a freer and more mature appreciation of what in fact as a Catholic he possessed.

The eviction of his tenants for refusing to renounce their faith by the apostate MacDonald of Boisdale brought the beginnings of Highland emigration across the Atlantic. MacDonald of Glenaladale initiated the scheme, ultimately selling all his estates in order to pay for land for their settlement, and following the other emigrants to St John's Island. Bishop Hay sent out an appeal, which was supported by Bishop Challoner who raised funds in England. Their activities frightened some of the lairds who, fearing the loss of their own tenants, compelled Boisdale to give up his unsuccessful efforts to extend the Reformation. The emigrants suffered great hardships, to which they were only too well accustomed.

For some twenty years, although he outlived him by a dozen more, Bishop Hay had as his coadjutor Bishop John Geddes, whose personality is perhaps the most warmly attractive of any amongst the fine tradition of eighteenth-century Scottish bishops. It was Bishop Geddes who became the helpful and understanding friend of Robert Burns and whom the poet described as the finest Christian minister he had ever known. Where Bishop Hay was somewhat rigorous, Bishop Geddes was expansive, extremely popular in polite and cultured society, learned and of the widest interests. Bishop Hay was adamant in maintaining austerity in Catholic practice, and, even although for his own relaxation he played the fiddle himself, refused to allow music in church. He was criticized by a younger generation of priests, while Bishop Geddes was criticized by an older generation for being too much the dandy. But, while they differed over details, the two bishops themselves remained always devoted friends. It is odd to think of

Bishop Geddes being considered latitudinarian when we read of his tremendous activity, which finally ruined his health so that he was bedridden for the last years of his life. He habitually made his journeys on foot, regularly walking to Glasgow from Edinburgh because he found these long walks gave him his only freedom from interruption for recollection and meditation. He enjoyed his walks, too, for the opportunity they gave him to visit old churches and castles and to maintain his interest in archaeology. *Ambula coram Deo* he chose as his motto.

More than any other individual, John Geddes prepared the way for the support that was given by the more humane and better-educated Scots of the time to move for the repeal of the penal laws; for in him they saw a man who, while his whole life and strength were vested in his religious belief, sustained a lively interest in history and scholarly studies, and a keen and practical appreciation of poetry and the arts; who was charming and helpful equally to Catholic and Protestant; who would go to great pains to bring comfort to a condemned murderer, and be a witty and always welcome guest at the erudite table of Lord Monboddo.

Before his consecration, John Geddes had been sent to Madrid to reorganize the Scots College there. Founded by a Scottish Colonel in the Spanish service, Colonel William Sempill, in 1627, the College had been the least useful of our national colleges abroad, its history vexed by litigation with the Spanish authorities over funds. John Geddes transferred it to Valladolid and started it there on a much better footing.

The other colleges for the Scottish mission were at Rome, Douai and Paris. For much of the time the two former were administered by the Jesuits. All three were shut down under the French revolutionaries. Douai and Paris were never revived, but Rome was reopened in 1820 by Abbé Paul Macpherson. Abbé Paul is another outstanding figure in penal Scotland. Born a crofter's son in the Braes of Glenlivet, he went, at the age of thirteen, with one companion of twelve, to the College at Rome in 1770. With the suppression of the Jesuits in 1773, the administration of the College passed into the rather unsatisfactory hands of Italian seculars, and later, owing to ill-health, young Macpherson was sent to Valladolid to complete his training. After fourteen years on the Scottish mission he was given the important post of agent in Rome. Here his activities to get the College put again into Scottish hands were violently interrupted by the French occupation. Abbé Macpherson acted with great tenacity and courage, escaping in charge of twenty-two students, Scots, English and Irish, through Europe. In London, to his surprise, he was welcomed as a hero, interviewed by Cabinet Ministers and presented to the Prince of Wales. He returned to Rome as soon as he could to rescue the Scottish property there, securing the help of a fellow Scot in Cardinal Erskine. He underwent great danger and difficulty but achieved much, and spent his spare time doing research into the history of the Scottish mission. He was expelled, but came back to Rome once more, even at one time being asked by the British Government to help in the rescue of the Pope from his French captors. His life is a fascinating byway of history, lit by his own courage, activity and humour, spent between his beloved Glenlivet and the Eternal City. He gave away everything he had, to the poor of Glenlivet and to the College which he successfully re-established, dying as its Rector at the age of ninety.

CHAPTER XII

TOWARDS EMANCIPATION

"THERE is no more humiliating chapter in our history and legislation than these penal statutes against the downtrodden Romanists. . . . They were to be a proscribed and outcast race, denied not only the rights of fellow citizens, but the charity which is generally extended to the most worthless of our fellow creatures." The history of the Church in penal times is inevitably largely concerned with the priests of the mission, but there were always many thousands of layfolk who shared the persecution epitomized in those words by the Presbyterian historian, Dr John Cunningham.

Because the State was reluctant to make overt martyrs, the idea is sometimes held that there was a lack of constancy and heroism on the part of Scottish Catholics. This was not the case. There were always those who made heroic resistance. Although the death penalty was habitually reduced to banishment, such banishment to a foreign country, in a state of penury, stripped of possessions, might prove a slow death, and some of those consigned to prison were certainly not encouraged to come out alive.

Papists were forbidden to take employment themselves or to employ others. Their houses could be broken into and robbed without redress. Fines and penalties brought many families to ruin. There are tinkers in Scotland today who come of families driven to take to the road for their faith. Every now and again the execrated ornaments of the Church would be discovered, to be carried through the streets in mocking procession, the common hangman wearing the priest's vestments, the crucifix jeered at and spat upon and finally burnt with the other "baubles" at a mercat cross that had been given a fresh significance. Catholic marriages were not recognized, so that husband and wife could

be branded and savagely punished as fornicators. Formal excommunication by the Church of Scotland carried with it the
whole penalties of outlawry, leaving man and woman the defence-
less victim of any crime or violence. Sentence of death and the
drama of execution make a mark where, as was appreciated by the
persecutors, destitution is only ignominy.

Inevitably, Scotland lost many of the best of her people by
emigration during the two and a half centuries between the
Reformation and the repeal of the penal laws. Some went to
Ireland, but most went to the Continent where, if there was
nothing else, there was always a demand for soldiers. Such of the
noble families as remained Catholic might do so only by taking
little or no part in public affairs, withdrawing into their castles
like that Earl of Nithsdale who lived quietly, constructing and
adorning "the dainty fabric of his new lodging" at Caerlaverock.
There was little else they could contribute to the common good
of their country.

Two eighteenth-century Scottish Catholics who obtained
distinction beyond their own country may be mentioned if not
as being typical, at least as revealing the lot imposed upon the
lives of cradle-Catholic and convert in that time.

James Gibb, whose name is better known to fame in its Angli-
cized version of Gibbs, was born of a Catholic family in Aberdeen
in 1682. The story goes that during the brief amnesty under
James VII, James's father had the temerity to name two ugly
dogs Luther and Calvin, and for this, at the Revolution, he was
brought before the magistrates and, although the dogs it was that
died at the hands of the public hangman, their owner and his
family were heavily penalized. After 1700, when the system of
rewards for informers made life even more difficult for the
Catholics, James left the country. He might have become a
mission priest, for he studied for a time at the Scots College in
Rome. But it was a time in which, for a few years, the College
was most unfortunately under the rule of two quite unsuitable
principals, Italian Jesuits. Under their tyrannical régime there
were many failures in vocations, even apostasies. In 1705 only
three students were left and poor Bishop Nicolson was com-

plaining that due to the mismanagement the Roman College had
not sent him a single priest for five years. James Gibbs, like most of
his fellow students, left without being ordained. He lived in
Rome for a time, studying architecture, and came to London in
1709. In the ensuing years he built up a practice as one of the
leading architects of his day. His talents apart, he had everything
against him, his nationality, his known Jacobite sympathies in the
past, and his faith. He gave an English form to his name, renounced
politics, and lapsed as a Catholic, and so gained the opportunity
he desired for the practice of his art. He was responsible for
famous buildings at Oxford and Cambridge, published a standard
book of architectural designs, and with the building of St Martin-
in-the-Fields and other churches may be said to be the chief
begetter, by way of Wren, of the classical architecture of Angli-
canism as practised in colonial America as well as in Britain. In
Scotland he built one church, that of St Nicholas in Aberdeen. By
the end of his life he had come back to his faith. Some fellow
Scottish Catholics in London were his close friends, the painter
Cosmo Alexander, and a family of Kerrs who after his death
transmitted a legacy to the Scottish mission—such legacies had,
of course, to be paid in a roundabout way. If a little lacking in
heroism, James Gibbs was a worthy man and an excellent
architect who in happier times might have served his own
country well.

No hero either, one who led a much less worthy life but, if
such comparison may be made, even more excellent as a writer
of prose than James Gibbs as an architect, was James Boswell,
author of one of the greatest biographies ever written. It is now
known that in his youth Boswell was received into the Church
and, so great was the superstitious dread aroused by such a step
at that time even in the trained mind of a judge, that his
father, Lord Auchinleck, deliberately vitiated his son's character,
making a rake of him under the influence of the Earl of Eglinton,
in order to wean him from "idolatry". The agony of a mind that
even after years of dissipation remained fantastically clear and
honest breaks out in Boswell's journals as he sneaks off to Mass at
one of the embassy chapels in London, or disputes points of

theology with Dr Johnson. In his will he asked for prayers for his soul in a passage which was suppressed by his executors, for to Protestants then, whether Scots or English, the idea that such prayers had any value ranked high amongst the odious tenets of Catholic credulity.

Bishop Hay, the old, austere, canny prelate, was the focal figure in the emergence of the Catholics of Scotland, and, as it happened, in England too, from the law-hewn catacombs into which they had been thrust. A Protestant, Sir John Dalrymple, "a man of exceedingly good heart", becoming on friendly terms with his fellow Scots amongst the Catholics in Paris, was deeply struck with the folly and injustice of the penal laws. Sir John was a Baron of Exchequer, highly respected in Ministerial circles, and his first achievement was on behalf of Ireland, where concessions were granted so that Catholic regiments could be raised there. The fear of a French war, and the defeat of Burgoyne by Americans who offered freedom and sanctuary to the persecuted Catholics of Britain, strengthened Sir John's case. He came to Edinburgh, where Bishop Hay told him that, the numbers and property of the Scottish Catholics being so small, their cause could best be served by uniting it with that of the English Catholics. Bishop Hay put him in touch with Bishop Challoner, and in 1778 the cause of Catholic Emancipation was launched.

Unfortunately the English Catholic nobility showed themselves disloyal to their Scottish fellows, and indeed to their own bishops, and secured their own Relief Bill without including Scotland in the measure. Bishop Douglas records a conversation that took place between Hay and Challoner at this time.

> Bishop Hay dining with Bishop Challoner, told him of the affront he had received from the noblemen. . . . B. Challoner paused and then spoke of the disregard for their clergy, and that many of them would fall off from their religion. B. Hay lamented this because, as many of them supported priests and chapels, religion would suffer by the apostasy. On which the Bishop again paused, then said, "There will be a new people". This was considered by Bishop Hay as a prediction of what would take place in a few years.

It does indeed remain a sad fact that after emancipation the representatives of many English families, who had held the faith with the greatest courage and constancy under persecution, apostatized: but from the still-oppressed people of Ireland there came "a new people".

The delay in obtaining a Scottish Relief Bill proved tragic. The General Assembly of 1778 flared up into hysteria. As usual, it was amongst "the most ignorant and uneducated of the people" that opposition reached its crescendo, with an organization called "Friends of the Protestant Interest". Glasgow, then with a mere score of poor Highland Catholics, saw the first outbreak of violence, the rabbling of Fr Menzies and his congregation at Sunday Mass. Educated Protestants, such as the great Principal Robertson of Edinburgh, who were known to favour the Bill, were mobbed and threatened with murder, and known Catholics were hardly safe in the streets. Early in 1779 the Scottish Relief Bill was withdrawn by an apprehensive Government. Even so, Bishop Hay returned from London on February 2nd to find his house and his chapel in the Blackfriars Wynd in the very process of being sacked. Mercifully he was not recognized and was able to walk quietly away from the pillage, in which his precious library of ten thousand volumes was totally destroyed. Bishop Hay's long insistence upon the Catholics remaining unobtrusive was shown to have been only too well justified. To John Geddes, then in Valladolid, he wrote: "To you, my dear friend, who know the secrets of my soul, I may tell my mind without restraint, because I know it will give you pleasure. I have not had one moment's concern or regret on the occasion, nor a single motion of resentment against our persecutors. I pity them; I pray for them; and I am as willing to give them my person as my property, if God should so please. May His blessed will be done in me continually."

Nothing could better have served the Catholic cause than this spiritual constancy of the great bishop: his profound and godly goodness brought him the support of all men capable of recognizing it. In Parliament Edmund Burke was inspired to make one of his brilliant orations, but here Walpole's "Lunatic Apostle of

Protestantism" rose in opposition, and a year later he, Lord George Gordon, led the London mob in those anti-Catholic riots that set the city ablaze, caused the slaughter of hundreds of people, and seriously shook the complacency of the eighteenth century in its belief in the supremacy of reason as the motive force in human conduct.

It was not until 1793 that the Scottish Catholics received any mitigation of their state. The immediate cause was the claim by his nearest Protestant relative to the estates of a Galloway laird, George Maxwell of Munches. Maxwell consulted Bishop Geddes, who enlisted the sympathetic help of the leading Edinburgh lawyers. The Lord Advocate was prepared to present a Bill in Parliament for the safeguarding of Catholic property, but Bishop Geddes was able, on the strength of his great personal popularity, to get the necessary support from leading Protestants in the capital for a more far-reaching measure. The Government was reassured, the Bill was brought forward without opposition and became law, receiving the royal signature on June 3rd.

Although fears had been felt up to the last moment that the Act would awaken the old hideous hostility, it was instead welcomed throughout a country that had at last grown somewhat weary of bigotry. The Act did not of course give the Catholic population parity with Protestants: it was many years yet before Catholics could vote or sit in Parliament, become officers in the Army or the Navy, legally teach in schools, or marry elsewhere than in a Protestant church. Nevertheless the change in their status was enormous. Overnight, Catholics ceased to be constitutional felons, and their Protestant neighbours could extend an open friendship that many had hesitated to show them before.

Although Catholics were still emigrating from the Highlands, many going to Nova Scotia, driven forth largely by chiefs who had sacrificed principles of leadership and responsibility for a simple rapacity, a new outlet was opening for them with the advent of the Industrial Age. The horrors that that age brought in its train make it hard to see that it brought also, first to the Highlanders and then to a starving Irish peasantry, at least a chance of continued existence, and at first, through the benevolence of such employers as David Dale, conditions not always bad. About the time of the Scottish Relief Act we find Bishop Hay writing enthusiastically of the demand for labour being so great in the Glasgow factories that the manufacturers had agreed to assist with the support of a Catholic chapel and priest. Fr MacDonell was the priest in question and he was himself responsible for recruiting labour and negotiating with David Dale. The Irish immigration was just beginning, although their uninhibited Catholicism was looked at askance by the Scots as being too liable to attract unwelcome attentions.

The French Wars brought an industrial slump which quickly changed the balance, and the unemployed workers tasted the greater bitterness of urban poverty. Fr MacDonell now tried to obtain Government sanction for the raising of a Catholic Regiment, the Glengarry Fencibles. His restless nature made him better adapted to initiating projects than to consolidating them, and his long absences from his parochial work in Glasgow made him a source of trial to his bishop. Eventually as chaplain to his regiment Fr MacDonell went to Canada, where he later became first Bishop of Kingston, Ontario, and it was left to his successor, Fr John Farquharson, actually to build the first post-Reformation Catholic chapel in Glasgow, opened in 1797. It was a humble upper-chamber, reached by an outside stair with the priest's quarters on the ground floor, the place of worship for a congregation that had already risen to hundreds, and was to grow steadily until Glasgow was the main centre of Catholicism in Scotland.

Meanwhile the overseeing of all this development still lay with Bishop Hay, who into the beginning of the nineteenth century was regaling children and seminarians with wonderfully-told stories of the '45, and of his own father's escape during the '15. For a time, before ill-health forced Bishop Geddes to leave Edinburgh, Bishop Hay was back at Scalan, combining episcopal and parochial duties with the administration of the little college (now, with the suppression of the Continental Seminaries, vital to the mission). He still travelled far, on foot or on horseback, evangelizing and celebrating Mass. Always he took with him his medicines, for his early training enabled him to minister to body as well as to soul. Nor were his attentions confined to his own people. Fr Carmichael has left the following account of an incident that took place while he was a boy at Scalan:

> I can never forget one case I witnessed at the seminary. The good Bishop after the community evening prayers, at which he always attended, begged our prayers for an afflicted woman, for whom he was to offer up his Mass next morning. A report went out among us that she was possessed or "obsessed". The woman appeared in the oratory next morning with her husband, both of them Protestants, I think from Kildrummy. He was a decent countryman and seemed much dejected. Immediately after Mass the Bishop began the exorcism of the Church, the woman kneeling before him. At first she was tolerably calm, though a little restless, till he came to the words *dic mihi nomen*—tell me thy name, when all of a sudden she started up quite furiously, so that we little fellows looked quite anxiously at the door of the small chapel, which was shut, or probably some of us would have made our escape. With the most commanding and majestic mien I ever saw in man, the Bishop commanded her in the name of Jesus Christ to kneel down. She instantly obeyed and several times, when, with similar fury, she again attempted to rise, the same order, given in the same all-powerful name, and repeated, if possible, with more majestic energy and authority, always brought her to her knees again, until at last, by the time the exorcisms were completed, she became quite calm. She returned home perfectly cured, and many years afterwards I heard that her husband was very anxious to be instructed and received into the Catholic Church; but I am afraid that his distance from any priest prevented this.

Impoverished by conditions in Rome, the Church in Scotland was actually aided for a few years by a Government grant, obtained through the renewed good offices of Sir John Dalrymple and given the approbation of Mr Secretary Dundas with a warm tribute to that "pious, loyal and respectable body of men ... the Roman Catholic clergy of Scotland".

It was an astonishing change in the nation's attitude from the days when George Hay outlawed himself by embracing the ancient faith. He lived to supervise the founding of a new and larger college at Aquhorties on Donside. He wrote books of devotion much read in their day and translated into various languages. At last, at the age of eighty-three, the old bishop died on October 11th, 1811, having attended the birth of a new phase in the Church's life.

J

CHAPTER XIII

BELIEFS

IN the literature of Scottish Presbyterianism there is dis-
appointingly little that gives us any deep insight into the
spirituality of those of its members more able, or more concerned, to express themselves. Largely it is a literature that suffers
from a defensive polemical cast, a preoccupation with Church
politics and byways of argument over issues that have long since
lost their importance. A slightly oppressive puritanism, and a
general failure to reach a literary level of a standard that does not
rapidly date, further impoverish the written output of Presbyterianism. Yet, in spite of all the inhibiting elements in Calvinism,
we know that within its fold there have been and still are in-
numerable people whose spiritual life is real and profound.

Calvin of course derived his spirituality directly from a particular school of French Catholic theologians, just as Luther went to
some of the older German mystics for his sources. To the Catholic
it seems that the withdrawal of spiritual ideas from the sanctuary
of the Church leaves them victim to all kinds of error. This is
not to suggest that kindred errors are not to be found within the
Church, whose spokesmen have constantly had to attack manifestations of Illuminism or Quietism, and often in the condemning
of one excess may tend to stimulate another. Sometimes everything of thought seems in chaos, and only the immutable sacraments have sustained a, perhaps shaky, ethical code, and provided
a persistent spiritual focus. But these sacraments, the Mystical
Body of Christ that is the Church, give the Catholic a continuity
of faith and a secure mystical basis for his prayer. Outside the
Church men of lofty motive and spiritual insight have often
criticized her for rigidity, for the imposing of forms upon what
should be a free intimacy between man and his Maker. They have

failed to appreciate man's imperative need, emphasized by our Lord himself, for a law and an order, and how his very human potential imposes more intractable limits upon his freedom unless it is controlled, limited by his acceptance of that law. Within the Church, whatever the errors, the betrayals, or the vagaries of individual priests, the law stands as a reality. Outside the Church, as we have seen, the imposition of a code to replace her law quickly becomes needful to any corporate body of Christians. The new code will base itself, more or less, upon Catholic doctrine, and then burden itself with departures from it reflecting temporary enthusiasms that become increasingly irksome to succeeding generations. In the case of the Church of Scotland her doctrine was codified in the Westminster Confession whose tenets are no longer held complete by more than a quite insignificant minority of ministry and laity, if not indeed only amongst members of splinter-groups. Since it is felt it would be sacrilege, or a sign of weakness, to alter "one jot or tittle" of the Westminster Confession, the result has been to impose the need for a doctrinal indifference very remote from the attitude prevailing in the earlier history of the Reformed Church; an original insistence upon the demand of reason has given place to the claim that reason is not of major importance, that it does not matter how a man thinks, it is how he acts, perhaps even sometimes only how he feels, that counts. There is, of course, an element of truth in this: many men are muddled thinkers who act by better lights than their reason would seem to propose: but it is not the truth in whose cause the Protestant leaders claimed to establish their churches.[1]

Sometimes the effort of reconciling the hyper-aristocratic doctrine of predestination and the other inflexibilities of the Westminster Confession has proved too terrible a strain, as was the case with that brilliant and intrinsically noble and lovable figure, Hugh Miller, who, after his intellectual conflicts had

[1] In Scotland, with its many divisions of Protestantism, the tribute is sometimes paid to a person that "he is better than his religion". And how often it is true! The Catholic can only be humbled in the knowledge that he is never as good as his religion.

driven him into pathetically scurrilous attacks upon the Catholics, took his own life. But commonly growth in spirituality brings the individual Presbyterian back towards that same apostolic Christianity which, while claimed as their aim by the original Reformers, abides still, as it always has despite the failures of her members, in the Church of Rome, and is expressed in the persons of her saints, Francis of Assisi, Teresa of Avila, Thomas More, each giving the emphasis of his or her own character to the unifying motif of the apostolate. With a little knowledge of the facts of history it is impossible to include within a like classification John Knox or many at least of the brave, unhappy and turbulent "martyrs of the Covenant". It is inevitably more likely that we shall find the finest personalities of Presbyterianism rather amongst those who did not have to justify the flaws in their creed by violent conduct or intellectual wrestling, but for whom a more hidden life left them free to approach God in the privacy of a prayer that need not always even be vocal but that in Scotland has at times notably expressed the truth *laborare est orare*. These are people many of whom we still meet amongst our Presbyterian neighbours, and it is they and their predecessors whose Christianity has latterly safeguarded so much of what is best in our nation.

These are qualities that embrace that "mist of love, real Scottish love, reticent but deep and strong, full of pathos and prayer", evoked not only in these words but in her whole life by Mary Slessor, the Dundee mill-girl who became the heroic missionary of Calabar. Both Mary Slessor and David Livingstone were members of independent Presbyterian churches and early started employment in grim Victorian factories, until, as David Livingstone expressed it, "in the glow of love which Christianity inspires I soon resolved to devote my life to the alleviation of human misery". Livingstone went on to his great achievements in Africa, which included the suppression of the terrible slave-trade. Such work precludes narrowness, and Livingstone wrote with approbation of the work of the earlier Jesuit settlements in Portuguese territory.

Presbyterianism has many other striking exponents of the Christian ideal, chiefly, of course, unknown to fame, but deserving to be remembered. We may recognize one in the Rev. Mr MacDonald, minister of Ferintosh, appreciatively recalled in the *Memorabilia Domestica* of the Rev. Donald Sage. In the early part of the last century ardent ministers crossed to Ireland on missions to the destitute Catholic peasantry. Zealous but brash, they larded their Gospel teaching with abuse of the Pope and the Mass, and felt themselves heroic martyrs in the true tradition of the Covenanters when they provoked anger and even violence amongst hearers to whom this might well have seemed the last straw. But Mr MacDonald, driven to embark on his mission because in his simplicity he believed the Gospel "to be the only moral, spiritual, and even political panacea for all the evils which lay so heavily upon the poor Irish", kept to the Gospel, avoiding all controversy and, speaking in Gaelic, "preached the doctrines of the Cross in their divine and majestic simplicity". His transparent charity brought him a reception accorded to no other of these missionaries, and Donald Sage records: "Through the whole of his itinerancy in Ireland his fame always preceded him; he was never without a crowd and a welcome, and whether he travelled by day or by night he was equally safe. The wildest and most lawless of the Popish mob in Ireland, be they 'White-boys' or 'Peep-o'-Day-boys', however much in use and wont to fight with others or among themselves, were under a law of amity and good behaviour towards this Irish-speaking, Scottish preacher. So far were they from injuring or annoying him that, if any difficulty arose to his onward progress from the state of the road, or any danger to his person were threatened by those who did not know him, they were ready to come to his rescue." And Donald Sage adds: "Not so, however, did it fare with other preachers travelling through those same districts for similar purposes".

John Bethune, who was born in 1810 and died before he was thirty, was a Fife farmhand whose brief life is described for us by his brother, Alexander, who shared his poverty and hardship and himself died only a year or two later. The two brothers, self-educated, wrote stories of rustic life of the time, and John a number of poems. He was not a poet of any major talent, and his use of an English that was not his spoken tongue constrains his expression, but he was a genuine poet and able at times to convey profundity of experience. In particular his poems on the Presbyterian Sacrament reveal a religious experience quite outside self-conscious and doctrinaire solemnity and express the joy of spiritual communion in a manner most Catholic. In this he reveals clearly, with the gift of the poet, the underlying Catholic, universal Christianity that survived all the knotted nervous controversy of Presbyterianism, and, particularly in the lives of the simple, reached that true spirituality, that very glorying in God in pursuit of which John Calvin so tragically broke the unity of the Church and led generations into the wilderness of intellectual confusion.

Exceptionally revealing, not only of this spirituality but also in its picture of humble life in the early part of the last century, are the memoirs of Mrs Janet Bathgate. Under the title *Aunt Janet's Legacy*, her autobiography appeared in the closing years of the century when she was a very old lady. Although popular at the time, it has long been forgotten despite its interest as a firsthand account of social conditions. Yet its particular merit is the fine timbre of its observation, and despite a certain use of conventional expression, the spiritual growth it traces.

Janet was born the daughter of a ploughman in the Border country. Her parents were devout Presbyterians, of a kind then often called Cameronians, although the association commonly overlooked the grim violence of the seventeenth-century Covenanter, Richard Cameron. The Covenanters, of course, were their heroes, but, if their knowledge of history was simply what they could learn from writings that were unrestrained propaganda, what they respected and cherished were those best facets of the victims of the "killing times", their staunchness under persecution. The Church of Rome was quite simply identified with the devil, and they knew nothing whatever about it. But the tenor of their faith as described by Janet, despite a certain narrowness bred partly of straitened circumstances, is essentially away from hardness. She recalls her father saying when his gudewife exhorted the doctrine of a celebrated apologist for predestination, "though I love you and reverence Thomas

Boston, yet I have more faith in prayer than in election". His wife maintained her position by arguing: "But, gudeman, a praying person is Christian evidence; for, ye ken, reprobates canna pray".

They loved their countryside, the low-lying hills and the broad waters of St Mary's Loch, and as an infant Janet made herself a little flower-garden. When only seven she went out to service, working from dawn to dark for an old lady, a shepherd's mother, in a solitary cottage in the hills at Hartleap. She was harshly treated, but her gentle faith was her support, even although by her later verdict upon herself "as yet she did not know what it was to pray, but she did what she knew to be right at the time, and her conscience was at rest". There are moving accounts of the child learning to read largely by her own efforts, and teaching herself to write as she herded the cattle, pricking with a pin a letter to her parents.

Janet later went into service with the Duke of Buccleuch's chamberlain at Dalkeith. She devotedly nursed an ailing child night and day for three years, harming her own health, but when her mother remonstrated replying only, "God has called me to this work and I will not give it up; I will nurse my darling boy while he requires it. If he dies, I will die with him. And, dear mother, you know that love makes labour light."

There follows Janet's marriage to a saddler, four years of happiness despite poverty and much ill-health, and then at last her young husband hints to her that his sickness is a consumption of which he is dying. Incredulous, she tries to take his mind from himself.

"Shall I read you", she says, "a little of John Knox's *History of the Reformation* or a bit from *Brainerd's Life*, or some other good book?"

"My dear", he replied, "I have lost all taste for such books; I find more help for my spirit in the Gospel of St John than in all the books I possess or have ever read. I have seen there that many of our ideas are wrong as regards the work of Christ; I have come to see that Christ did not purchase the love of the Father, as I had thought, but that He came to reveal it. How we have misunderstood the meaning of the words that Christ spoke—God so loved the world that he *gave* his only begotten Son, that whosoever believeth in Him should have everlasting life. I am just beginning to see the glory of God in the face of Jesus Christ as I have not seen it before, and to understand how it is that—to know God, and Jesus Christ whom He has sent, is life eternal."[1]

Left a widow and destitute, struggling to support herself by sewing, it was suggested to Janet that she might give lessons to two or three small girls. She protested that she had never had more than six weeks schooling herself and felt it would be "the very height of presumption" for her to try to teach. But the following Monday brings a rap at the door, the visitor a wee lassie with stool and book and cloth for stitching, holding out tuppence, saying, "I am come to your school and this is my school wages".

The child is so disappointed when she denies that she has a school that Janet consents to take her in for the week. But by the Saturday she finds she has nine pupils, and on the following Monday eighteen scholars arrive, each with tuppence for fee.

At this point in her life Janet Bathgate brings her own story to a close. After her death a sequel was published giving a more summary account of her life after the year 1835. It was a time when the claim that salvation was open to all was beginning to be one of the causes of schism. The Rev. McLeod Campbell was deposed by the General Assembly of the Church of Scotland for preaching "the universality of God's love to mankind and of Christ's atonement for sin", and a few years later the Rev. James Morison of Kilmarnock was deposed on similar grounds by the United Secession Church. Having been employed to run a larger school near Penicuik, Janet began holding Sunday after-

---

[1] It should be remarked that Knox's *History* did not then circulate in a complete text. Many of his more violent and patently unchristian expressions of opinion were excised. St John's Gospel was still and for long after little countenanced by the more orthodox Presbyterians.

noon religious meetings there which with their kindlier, although
very pure and simple doctrine, became increasingly popular,
until she fell under the censure of the local ministers. The old
mob spirit that Hume defined as John Knox's particular con-
tribution to religion in Scotland was woken, there was a riot,
and the devoted and generally much-loved schoolmistress was
burnt in effigy. Later, she married again and went to Glasgow
where she became a member of Mr McLeod Campbell's Independent congregation.

In its more austere form Calvinism came late to the West
Highlands, where many of the Protestant clans long favoured
episcopacy. In the seventeenth century when the Parson of
Kintail was ousted by the ascendant Presbyterians and, going to
the Continent, became a Catholic and a priest, he returned to
convert many of his Macrae clansmen and establish the most
northerly Catholic outpost. There is a delightful description of
the happy life in the Isle of Skye at the beginning of the nineteenth century left by one of the Mackinnon family, those tacks-
men of Coirechatachan whose hospitality gave such satisfaction
to Johnson and Boswell. But on returning from India towards the
middle of the century, Kenneth Mackinnon deplored a big change
in the influence of religion, with fierce doctrinal disputes and with
social enjoyment under a cloud. This despondency was at least
largely due to the indifference shown to the area by the London
Government and the unrelieved destitution promoted by the
lifting of the duty upon barilla imports, which made fortunes
for the soap-manufacturers but brought utter ruin to Highlanders
dependent upon kelp-burning. Landlords sought to recoup
themselves by evicting their tenants in favour of sheep, breaking
ancient rights of tenure. A church ministry which under patron-
age tended to be biased in the landlords' favour, chose to see their
action as the judgment of God, not to be resisted. It was from the
Free Churches, who had no such allegiance, that the crofters
received more sympathy, and this, with the tendency of poverty
and destitution to seek solace and strength in austerity, made the
Highland area, which had been the last to feel its effects, also the
last stronghold of Calvinist puritanism.

One tragedy of the confined and suspicious Calvinist faith with its overtones of arbitrary election, still held amongst the Secession churches, is its inflexibility. While it may be sustained amongst a peasant society that asks little more than subsistence, and within a simple orbit can be mollified into gentleness and spirituality, it can make little resistance to a worldliness towards which its attitude can only be fiercely negative. It is a sad but inescapable fact that those areas where the Seceders are strongest are also those which produce an unhappily dissolute type of young man who, having rejected, or feeling hopelessly unworthy of the exalted but limited standards of his elders, tends to become a reckless outcast. Even in the Established Church in the West Highlands it is common for very few young men to presume to come forward for their Church's sacrament, for there is no confession or absolution open to them.

In a household in which the reading matter is confined to the Bible, to a few biographies of exceptionally irresilient divines, and to a Secession magazine that in stately old-world prose regularly resurrects Montrose and Sir Walter Scott in order to castigate them for their attitude to the Covenanters, the impact of the contemporary newspaper, with its pin-up girls, its enthusiasm for crime and its emphases upon gambling and good-timing, may readily be appreciated. There is no easily discernible compromise. The choice is liable to lie between complete religious conformity and, more usually, a violent rejection that may be accompanied by an embittering sense of guilt.

The tragedy is rooted in the loss of the concept of a loving God. It is no new problem. All the religions of the world have had to face the question of God's attitude to man, which inevitably determines man's attitude to God. The mystical religions of the East, although early convinced of the immortality of the soul, have sometimes lacked altogether a belief in God, an attitude that seems strange to us. Yet both amongst Hindus and Buddhists devout men have found their way through love to the recognition of the Godhead. Conversely, the early Jews, whose religion was prophetic rather than mystical, were more convinced of God than of their own immortality. But it is in Christ that God's love is

made materially manifest to man, a love of man as body as well
as soul. When the human excess of Calvin in his pursuit of purity
of faith swept away the Body of Christ he mortally weakened
men's sense of his person. It was not unnatural that Calvin's
followers should tend to revert to a Jewish apprehensiveness
before their Creator.

Within the various folds of Scottish Presbyterianism the
individual is able to find his way, by the Scriptures, by prayer
and by love of others, to recognizing again the love of God that
is so hard to reconcile intellectually with belief in an arbitrary
salvation and in the innate evil of God's own material creation.
When men approach God humbly enough strange beliefs seem
to become largely irrelevant, at least to the individual who holds
them although they greatly constrain his powers of useful communication to his fellow men. Yet Samuel Rutherford, who was
largely responsible for drawing up the formidable dogmatic
stumbling-block of the Westminster Confession, was at times
able to express profound spiritual truth in phrases of a beautiful
simplicity. Some of these, culled from his letters by the "In-
dependents" of her day, were sent by Janet Bathgate to the man
whose life she had saved many years before when he was a little
sickly boy:

> Christ's cross is the sweetest burden that ever I bear; it is
> such a burden as wings are to a bird, or sails to a ship, to carry
> me forward to my harbour. . . . Hold fast Christ, but take his
> cross and himself cheerfully: Christ and his cross are not
> separable in this life, however they part at heaven's door. . . .
> That Christ and a sinner should be one, and share heaven
> between them, is the wonder of salvation: what more could
> love do?

CHAPTER XIV

RE-ESTABLISHMENT

SCOTLAND'S second great settlement from Ireland was very different from her first. To the eye of the imagination at least the first seems a lovely odyssey, a springtime of civilization, with shapely boats full of rough, hopeful, happy colonizers, swinging through the sounds between the gilded islands of the Hebrides. Some fighting there was, but a physical combat with quick death or new life for prize. Above all, some of the boats carried an unseen cargo, an alembic distilling far more than a young civilization, giving form and purpose to human goodness, reuniting it with the divine good. Then comes a man possessed and transfigured by this faith, a man stripped of all other attachment, and made thereby more apt and wise, more happy and confident than any of his fellow-voyagers. Columba is followed by other saints who come in like charity, careless of their own life and death, offering life beyond death to the people of their adopted country, and founding a simple but real and vigorous civilization that even in its pristine state lasted for many generations, and has left its legacy down the ages.

There was nothing romantic about the appalling living and dying conditions in and around Glasgow, the sweated labour, uncertain wages, the stink and filth and overcrowding which swallowed up the people who came from Ireland thirteen hundred years later. So much had happened between the days of the Celtic saints and the early nineteenth century. Bad things had grown up along with the good, enormous weeds and tares that sometimes seemed to overshadow all man's emancipation from paganism; a sacrifice of body and soul to new-fashioned idols of wealth and greed, with Christianity adapted to accommodate them, faith put away on the shelf, a comforting but unregarded possession not allowed to challenge the old deities in their new garbs. The schism between rich and poor had become so wide that the poor had little other right than the right to starve when their labour was not wanted; they were "another nation" and many of them were indeed of another nationality that left them wide open to disregard and contempt.

In their different ways both Scotland and Ireland had suffered from being the weaker and poorer neighbours of an extremely successful England. Ireland was overwhelmed first and, except in her religion, more completely. It would be hard to exaggerate the calculated misrule imposed on the Irish by English domination: the deliberate prevention of any balanced economy so that Ireland should always be subservient, a vassal state buying surplus English goods and having to pay with her agricultural produce even when this was in no sense surplus but desperately needed by the Irish themselves. Scotland gained a measure of compromise when she finally entered upon an incorporating union with the "auld enemy" in 1707. She was nominally an equal partner although, as those who had tried to hold out for a federal union had foretold, she was very quickly made aware of the inequality of having only a small minority vote in a distant Parliament. It was however still possible for Scots to show and to exercise initiative even within their own country, although there was a perhaps natural tendency for this to be checked when it looked like effectually rivalling English interests. Scotland had sacrificed her religion under active English influence in pre-union days. The religion she had accepted in its place she guarded jealously from English control, at least partly for the sake of her own self-esteem, although the battle for Scottish religious independence from England had been first fought and won long before the Reformation, when Rome had quashed the claims of York to religious superiority.

Many of the Irish came over in the first place as seasonal agricultural labour, and stayed on in order to earn in the factories money that they could send to their needy families. With the construction first of canals and then of the railways, a supply of Irish navvies became essential to the gathering momentum of the

Industrial Revolution. They were employed under appalling conditions of long hours, bad accommodation and low wages, money much of which was extorted from them by their having to buy necessities from stores owned or leased by their employers. They provided also labour for the factories, at times making themselves understandably unpopular with the native Scots because in their destitution they were willing to accept lower wages. They found, moreover, a Protestant populace to whom a centrifugal tenet of religion was all too much one of protest, a violent antipathy to the one certitude the Irish had, their faith; although it must be said that those who came from the Protestant plantations of Northern Ireland were even more bigoted against their Catholic fellow-countrymen. A sense of enmity on the part of the Catholics was inevitable, and with it went an innate lack of respect for the law and institutions of the adopted country, for English law in occupied Ireland had very largely been simply a weapon of oppression and therefore traditionally deserving only of contempt. Altogether the relationship of the new Irish immigrants with those who were so largely the descendants of their predecessors was ugly, twisted and forlorn, incomparably more vexed than the straightforward situation that faced the contemporaries of St Columba.

Circumstances of history furthermore complicated their relationship with those Scots who had kept the same faith. Scottish Catholics were a secret people, especially when they left the small predominantly Catholic areas. They had long learnt to keep as quiet as they could about their faith and to make such compromise as was possible. To the Irish their faith had been the one thing in which they could express themselves with some freedom: it had become the chief expression of their identity. Even those whose religion did not go very deep, indeed it would probably be true to say they in particular, were liable to be aggressive in their Catholicism, because it alone gave them certitude and a sense of unity. Meanwhile the bishops and most of the priests were Scots, largely from the north-east, constitutionally somewhat unsympathetic to Irish expansiveness.

When Fr Andrew Scott was appointed to the Glasgow mission

in 1805 his congregation numbered less than five hundred. Within a few years it had risen to three thousand and Fr Scott decided that he must built a church large enough to accommodate this constant increase. He was considered wildly ambitious when he projected his church of St Andrew's, now the Cathedral. The imposing size and architecture of the new church by the riverside evoked fierce indignation over the effrontery of "the Scarlet Woman" and "the Man of Sin" in thus desecrating a city of Protestantdom. Fr Scott was accused of building it on "the pennies of the poor", which indeed he had to do, but they were pennies freely offered by those who, if they could ill spare them, yet rejoiced to be able to do something in the cause of their own faith and identity. The attacks of the Protestant Press became so virulent and personal that at last Fr Scott was compelled to bring an action for libel, which realized a useful sum towards the building fund. St Andrew's was opened in 1816, and, built in the agreeable early Gothic Revival style of Gillespie Graham, was considered the largest and finest Catholic "chapel" in Britain.

By the time the Catholic Emancipation Act of 1829 had restored the status of British Catholics to one of almost complete equality with their fellows, Glasgow was the main centre of the faith in Scotland with twenty-five thousand in its congregations. It was about then that Fr Scott began to have to face concerted attacks from within his own fold. *The Glasgow Free Press* was the mouthpiece of the Irish immigrants, making heated claims that their interests were being neglected in favour of the small Scottish contingent. Fr Scott replied to these attacks caustically from his pulpit in St Andrew's, and is reputed to have said on one occasion, in his broad Banffshire dialect, "If yer nac please't wi' the way I dae for yer guid, whatfor dinna ye tak' a sail tae Rome, and see hoo ye come on at the Vatican, if ye ken whaur that is!" The claim that the dominant Irish element was not being consulted or allowed to share in the management of the temporalities of the Glasgow mission was echoed in immigrant papers in London and elsewhere. There was justice in it, although the attacks were expressed with a violence and bitterness that called for and received a rebuke from Rome. But it should be said that if Bishop

Scott, as he became in 1832, was hidebound in his administration, he and his clergy did not fail in their practical priesthood, but faced outbreaks of typhus and cholera to visit the sick and dying in the dreadful slum tenements, with great reeking middens at their doors, sometimes having to face at the same time the abuse of resentful Protestants.

The potato famine of the 1840s, which within a few years reduced the population of Ireland through starvation and emigration by more than the whole population of Scotland, swelled the numbers coming here with a people utterly embittered by the injustice under which they had been prevented by armed troops from eating the food they had produced in their own country, and who came to an unwelcoming Scotland and England only with resentment. It was no wonder if their attitude was intemperate. Within the Glasgow mission the situation of these displaced persons became more and more unhappy. The appointment of an Irish coadjutor bishop seemed only to increase the tension and disunion. An Apostolic Visitation was ordered by Rome, and made by Archbishop Manning of Westminster. As a result of his report an Englishman, thirled neither to the Scottish nor to the Irish interest, Mgr Charles Eyre, Vicar-General of Hexham and Newcastle, was appointed Administrator of the Scottish Western District in 1869, and, with the Restoration of the Scottish Hierarchy in 1878, first post-Reformation Archbishop of Glasgow.

Charles Eyre was a man of outstanding ability, with a tact and a goodness that enabled him to overcome difficulties that had seemed almost insuperable. In the thirty-three years of his episcopacy he completely healed the old rift within the Glasgow area, which he developed beyond recognition, the number of priests increasing from seventy-four to two hundred and thirty-four. He showed himself a really great administrator, bringing the discipline and organization that the rapid growth and changing circumstances demanded and whose lack had allowed for so much dissension. He founded many new parishes and schools, besides establishing St Peter's training college for priests, and, a wealthy man, put his private fortune at the service of the diocese. His episcopal administration became the model for the whole of the restored episcopate of Scotland. Archbishop Eyre came of an aristocratic recusant family in Yorkshire, and this in itself helped to present Catholicism in a new light to the socially-conscious burghers of Glasgow.

Indeed, the unfortunate Catholics, long associated with poverty, and latterly with slumdom and its concomitant evils, badly needed social prestige if they were to be allowed to take their part in, and so to influence for its good, the life of their country. Moreover, while the Church gives all honour to those whose vocation it is to embrace the ascetic ideal, she has never condemned the good things of the world in themselves but has seen all legitimate human activity, in the way of learning, of the graces of life and human relationships, as part of God's providence, capable in his service and therefore her concern.

To the English the "Second Spring", with which the great name of John Henry Newman is forever associated, brought a new conception of the faith so long proscribed. At the same time Scotland also had a number of converts whose position and attainments commanded respect from the established leaders of society. Among these was one of Newman's own closest friends, James Hope-Scott, a layman whose subsequent devoted service to the Church took many forms.

Gladstone, another lifelong friend, described Hope-Scott as "without doubt the most winning person of his day", and there are many tributes to his great personal charm and consideration for others. He was a Fellow of Merton College at an early age and, taking his position seriously, made studies into the origins and "idea" of a University which later inspired Newman's famous work. Indeed, after both had come into the Church it was at Hope-Scott's suggestion that Newman was charged with the establishing of the University of Ireland, and it was to him that Newman dedicated his *University Sketches* with the tribute:

To James R. Hope-Scott, Q.C., a name ever to be had in honour when universities are mentioned, for the zeal of his early researches, and the munificence of his later deeds, this

K

volume is inscribed, a tardy and unworthy memorial, on the part of its author, of the love and admiration of many eventful years. Dublin, October 28th, 1856.

Born of the celebrated Lowland family of Hope, once active supporters of John Knox, Hope-Scott married the grand-daughter of Sir Walter Scott, daughter of John Gibson Lockhart, Scott's rather fractious biographer, and, on her inheriting Abbotsford, added the surname Scott to his own. His wife was received into the Church shortly after him, and was herself an exceptional woman, described as "making her inner life, as far as possible, that of a religious". She and two of her children died with tragic suddenness all within two months. Hope-Scott married again, a daughter of the Duke of Norfolk.

He was a barrister by profession and gained a unique reputation for his work in the legislation then being framed for the development of the railways, pleading before the Parliamentary committees. By the time he retired, Hope-Scott was reputed to be in receipt of a hundred retaining fees from the various companies and interests involved. He liked the work partly because it was straight pleading that did not involve questions of conscience, partly because it only occupied half of each year. Although he worked a twelve-hour day while the committees were sitting, he was able to spend long holidays, first in travel, making friends with many distinguished men on the Continent, and later with his family. He bought properties in Mayo, at Hyères in France, and on Loch Shiel in the Highlands. The last he bought without having seen it, to prevent it falling into Protestant hands, and he did much for the native Catholic population there, building the church and school at Mingarry and the church at Glenuig. He also built his own house of Dorlin and gave valuable employment and stimulus in opening out roads where there had been none before. Both in Ireland and in France he assisted the Catholic life of his tenants and neighbours, and near Abbotsford he built the churches at Galashiels, Jedburgh and Kelso. The last of these was burnt down in an anti-Catholic riot in 1856, and the *Scotsman* had occasion to censure some stupid and bigoted remarks made by the Lord Justice-Clerk at the trial of some of the rioters. Highland priests in those days sometimes received as little as £12 for stipend, and Hope-Scott came generously to their support.

Throughout his life Hope-Scott used his large income in countless works of charity, both public and private. In 1836 the great Bishop Gillis had brought the first religious community to be established in Scotland since the Reformation to Edinburgh, Ursulines of Jesus, and Hope-Scott was their benefactor and is buried in the vault of St Margaret's Convent chapel. His legal knowledge and the universal respect in which he was held made his advice and assistance of great help during the gradual strengthening of the Catholic position in Britain.

Another convert was the third Marquess of Bute. With the death of his father in 1848 he inherited, as a child of six months, one of the largest fortunes in Britain. His mother died when he was still a boy and he was left in the care of guardians who were all staunch Protestants. Yet when he went to a preparatory school in England the headmaster wrote of him: "I was not surprised to find in him an admiration of the Covenanters and a hatred of Archbishop Sharpe" (Lord Bute retained an intolerance of Scottish Episcopalianism on the grounds of its Erastian origins), "but I was certainly startled to discover, on the other hand, a liking for the Romish priesthood and ceremonial. I shall, of course, do my best to bring him to sounder views."

But while he was still at Oxford, without having come into personal contact with any Catholics, the young Marquess announced his wish to be received into the Church. His reasons were characteristically scholarly and direct:

I came to see very clearly that the Reformation was in England and Scotland—I had not studied it elsewhere—the work neither of God nor of the people, its real authors being, in the former country, a lustful and tyrannical king, and in the latter, a pack of greedy, time-serving and unpatriotic nobles. (Almost the only real patriots in Scotland at that period were bishops like Elphinstone, Reid, and Dunbar.) I also convinced myself (1) that while the disorders rampant in the Church during the sixteenth century clamoured loudly for reform, they in no way justified apostasy and schism; and (2) that were

I personally to continue, under that or any other pretext, to remain outside the Catholic and Roman Church, I should be making myself an accomplice after the fact in a great national crime and the most indefensible act in history. And I refused to accept any such responsibility.

When, however, he announced his intention to his guardians there was something like pandemonium which, owing to his exalted wealth and position, reached as far as Queen Victoria herself. It was of course taken for granted that some undercover Jesuit had corrupted the young man. Yet, as his friend Abbot Hunter-Blair describes it:

The circumstances of the case were patent and simple. A young man of strong religious instincts, good parts, and studious habits, had, after much reading, grave consideration (and, it might be added, earnest prayer, but that was outside the public ken), come to the conclusion that the religion of the greater part of Christendom was right and that of the British minority wrong. And what made matters worse was that he had in his constitution so large a share of native Scottish tenacity, that there seemed no possibility of inducing him to change his mind. The obvious, and only alternative policy, was delay. Get him to put off the evil day, and all might yet be well. The *mot d'ordre* was accordingly given; and a united crusade was entered on by kinsfolk and acquaintance, guardians, curators, and tutors-at-law, the Chancellor and his myrmidons, the family solicitors, and finally the dons and tutors at Oxford, to extract from the prospective convert, at whatever cost, a promise not to act on his convictions at least until after attaining his majority. After that—well, anything might happen; and if during the interval of nearly two years he were to take to drink or gambling, to waste his substance on riotous living (like his unfortunate cousin), or generally to go to the devil—it would of course be very regrettable, but anyhow he would be rescued from Popery, and that was the only thing that really mattered.

Lord Bute finally consented very reluctantly to delay his reception until he came of age. This occurred in 1869 and the outburst to which it gave rise in the British Press makes amusing reading today. From the London *Times* down to the local *Buteman* rich veins of sarcasm, contempt or heavy warning, were struck. The *Scotsman* was an honourable exception, refusing to "taunt or reproach", maintaining that "even those who must deeply regret it must admit Lord Bute's change of religious opinion to be made at great sacrifice and under the influence only of conscience", which, however, was hardly borne out in the other writers of editorials who seemed determined that the young peer was either "of a weak, ductile and naturally superstitious mind", or morally "perverted", and that the Church of Rome could only have secured his allegiance by shameless machinations of "Jesuitism".

This outcry in the Press of less than a hundred years ago is interesting in showing how limited and ingrained Protestantism had become in Britain, so that to the common mind it still seemed inconceivable that any man, at least of position and education, could become Catholic by a conviction that was both sane and honest. But at least it was no longer a penal offence to be a Catholic. Lord Bute lived down the obloquy he had incurred, and became a popular personality in the country while always remaining independent in his views—although a Tory, he was sympathetic to Scottish Home Rule. He was devoted to his island of Bute and served it well, becoming Provost of Rothesay. He built and endowed churches and convents with the rather ornate taste in architecture of his time, and he applied a varied scholarship to, amongst other things, translating the Roman Breviary and supporting the intellectual *Scottish Review*. His translations of the hymns of St Thomas Aquinas are notably good. There remained in him a certain freshness of eccentricity perhaps in part due to the remoteness promoted by vast wealth. A very different world from that of Bishop Scott is evoked in such a passage as the following from one of Lord Bute's letters: "George Lane Fox was married to Miss Slade on Saturday. I gave her for a marriage present that rosary of emeralds you used to admire so much; and she at once wrote and asked my consent to its being altered into a necklace! which I refused to give."

Coming into the twentieth century, tremendous good was done to the prestige of the Catholics who were beginning to be a

force in University life in Glasgow by the accession to the staff
there of a remarkable Englishman, John Swinnerton Phillimore.
Phillimore was a man of immense intellectual distinction and a
personality that gained him the devoted friendship of G. K.
Chesterton and other leading figures of his time. The effect
upon a generation of Scots still liable to be bigoted with inherited
prejudice of coming "under the sway of a Catholic who was the
embodiment of all that was finest both intellectually and spirit-
ually in the whole western world" could, as Mr Colm Brogan
recalls, hardly be exaggerated. Yet even some chance words of a
man of the status and integrity of Phillimore, spoken at a school
prize-giving, were once interpreted as implying a papist plot to
infiltrate and turn the Universities into Catholic institutions, and
called forth a brief hysterical anti-Catholic campaign. A little
later the most distinguished member of the University staff in
Edinburgh, Sir Edmund Whittaker, a mathematician of world
repute and a man of great modesty and charm, became a Catholic.

Several of the religious orders and congregations had opened
houses in Scotland even before the restoration of the hierarchy
once more fully established the Church as part of the nation's
life. The Society of Jesus, which almost from its earliest days had
had a lively Scottish contingent, was active in both Edinburgh
and Glasgow. The Benedictines had taken over the old Hanoverian military fortress of Fort Augustus. Two newer congregations, the Passionists and the Redemptorists, were in Glasgow and Perth respectively. Franciscans opened a house in
Glasgow, later in Edinburgh. From no less than five centres the
Sisters of Mercy worked amongst the needy, and both the Sisters
of Charity and the Little Sisters of the Poor had more than one
house from which to carry on their patient works of charity.
Since 1878 there have been many other foundations. The Cistercians, whose ancient abbeys are amongst Scotland's most
imposing mediaeval ruins, have returned to Lothian. The
Dominican friars have an Edinburgh priory. There are Augustinians, Capuchins, White Fathers, Vincentians and Servites. The
mediaeval monastery of Pluscarden is once more the home of
monks, white-habited Benedictines of the Cassinese Congrega-

tion, brought there by a son of Lord Bute. Carmelites, leading an enclosed life of prayer and intercession, are amongst many orders of nuns who have now come to Scotland, and who include such teaching orders as the Society of the Sacred Heart and the Sisters of Notre Dame.

Education in Scotland had inevitably suffered a setback at the Reformation, with the loss of endowments and teachers. Gradually the Reformers built up a new system of parish schools, but, although in many ways Scottish education compared favourably with that of other countries, schools for long remained very inadequately distributed. In the Catholic areas they were used as a means of proselytism, and Catholics had great difficulty in educating their children elsewhere. The sons of the wealthier were often sent abroad, although this was strictly forbidden and penalized. In the remotest parts schools were occasionally established by Catholics, but always under threat of summary closure and the banishment of the teacher. Although the first Relief Act still banned Catholic schoolteachers, since there were no stated penalties attached a certain number were more or less openly active before the Emancipation Act of 1829. Thereafter strenuous steps were taken to establish schools wherever they were needed. Under certain conditions government grants were made available to some of the voluntary schools, which included Episcopalian schools as well as Catholic, but they could claim no assistance from the main source of educational revenue, the local rates, to which of course Catholics and Episcopalians were equally bound to contribute. Maintenance of their schools became a major problem, as Sir Compton Mackenzie records:

> The result was an always harassing anxiety for the Catholic priests who had to beg the money, a cruel handicap for the Catholic teachers who had to accept lower salaries than the State-paid teachers, a grinding burden upon the Catholic parents of children, who had to find the money, and most serious of all, a grave material injustice to the Catholic children themselves, who were less well taught and less well housed than their little Protestant brothers and sisters, and who therefore entered the world at a marked disadvantage with them.

The anomaly was brought to an end by a notably fair and enlightened piece of legislation, the Scottish Education Act of 1918, whereby the State purchased or leased the voluntary schools without prejudice to their religious teaching, raising the standard and establishing equality in educational opportunity and responsibility.

The greatest credit is due to those who framed the 1918 Act, but it is sad to have to recall that this honourable settlement of a just grievance provoked lingering outbursts of the old resentment. Of course the better-spirited and more humanely educated of Church of Scotland spokesmen applauded it, and only deplored the fact that their own Church had not maintained like supervision of Presbyterian schools. But there were others in whom bigotry vitiated the sense of both justice and Christian unity. A Committee of the General Assembly produced a document that called for the abolition of all religious tests for teachers "except a religious test which will prevent any member of a religious order, male or female, from teaching in State schools": suggesting that even the most virulent atheist was to be preferred to those orders who founded the whole education of the Western World, and who, in the sons of St Benedict, preserved and forwarded Christianity a thousand years before the Church of Scotland existed.

EPILOGUE

I WAS myself one of those whose curiosity brought them into the old High Street of Edinburgh, under the shadow of the High Kirk of St Giles, on a summer day in 1935. The Freedom of the City was to be given to the Prime Minister of Australia, Mr Lyons, who happened to be a Catholic. The hired agitator had reappeared amongst us, and, with all the ill-manners of self-righteousness, the leaders of Knox's "rascal multitude" chose the occasion for a demonstration. It was at a time, of course, when similar mobs were screaming Hitler into power to loose untold misery upon the world, and I remember bitterly the horror of seeing human beings, largely adolescents and women of a disappointed mien, possessed beyond the reach of reason, screaming and rushing, ready for murder, upon the car in which Archbishop Andrew Joseph MacDonald drove up to the City Chambers. Veneration of John Knox had once again inspired emulation of his tactics. This was "protest" and as such it was of the genesis of Protestantism. Whatsoever Protestantism had retained of Christianity, and in countless individuals we know that this has always comprehended much of its divine essence, it seemed to me then to exist in distinction only as a negation, a protest against something that it did not appear even to wish to understand.

It is only just to recall that very similar feelings were expressed by leading Protestants themselves at that time. Principal W. M. MacGregor stated unequivocally, "Sympathetic indignation is awakened and just-minded outsiders are driven to feel that, if Protestantism can be vindicated only in such crude ways, its day is nearly done."

But of course Protestantism has other and very different vindications: primarily in the lives of so many of its adherents. Only in so far as it is negative, productive of an anxious bigotry, can it serve no good.

I was not the only Protestant witness of those ugly scenes in the summer of 1935 who within a few years found himself no longer protestant, having progressively discovered how much of the stock picture of my country's history was mere myth. For in pre-Reformation days men were not put to death, nor even penalized by law, for holding Protestant views. A few were put to death for propagating those views, but, although except under spells of National-Socialist and Communist retrogression, such savagery is mercifully in abeyance today, all governments have a need and a duty to take some steps to check the spreading of ideas that they consider a threat to the State. That the ideas of the original Scottish Protestant propagandists, a number of whom are known to have been professional enemy agents, were a menace to the integrity of their country was only too well proven in the disasters that befell us at their hands. After the Reformation, on the other hand, so consistently claimed in Scotland as an intellectual liberation, men were persecuted, imprisoned and banished, not only for propagating ideas but for merely holding them. The Catholic whose views kept him from attending Protestant indoctrination was a felon; if he were found to possess crucifix or rosary if only for his most private devotions, he was treated as the most depraved and vicious of criminals. Either, then, the Catholics were diabolically evil, repository of ideas that even privately sustained were a menace to the noblest tenets of Presbyterianism, or the institutes of Presbyterianism in its heyday were negative, an expression of ignorance. And it did not seem reasonable to suppose that Catholics, so much of whose doctrine was retained as the core of all Protestant beliefs, were in fact diabolic.

Not of course that most of us are decisively influenced by historical reassessments. The process of conversion is never entirely intellectual, but involved with the whole man, body and mind and spirit. It is through the spirit that the gift of faith is ultimately to be received, and as such is beyond man's scope to claim but remains a mystery that humbles him in the smallness of the part that is his. Body and mind are less mysterious in the process of our finding a defined faith, but in Scotland four hundred years of misrepresentation, deliberate or made in all ignorance, have left many of her people with strangely distorted, superstitious ideas about the faith of their forefathers, the beliefs that remain those of the substantial majority of their fellow Christians.

In respect of the body, the celibacy of clergy and nuns seems to be an affront in the eyes of many Protestants. Yet to the Catholic the ideal of chastity is not seen as a puritanical condemnation of man's nature but rather as a supreme mark of respect whereby a perfect gift may be offered to God by those who are granted the grace to make it. Although it is only for the few, it remains an ideal without which it is far more difficult to realize a sexual equilibrium and that continence which is demanded of us in countless relationships, not least in matrimony. We know that uninhibited passion, far from being the liberation claimed by certain pseudo-scientific psychologists, is itself our most menacing inhibition, blinding rational judgments and constantly frustrating the full realization of our humanity.

The Church sees the sexual relationship sanctified in holy matrimony, in which it is part of a whole relationship between man and woman and, normally, children. As such, the potentials of matrimony are magnificent and its difficulties vast, since, exalted into a sacrament, it becomes a divine means to human perfection with all the demands upon us implied in the injunction of our Redeemer, *estote perfecti*.

How often when we were young were we told that Catholics "didn't mind sinning, because they could always go to confession, get forgiven, and then do it again"? This simple analysis carried with it a rather ingenuous implication that only Protestants could be honestly contrite. Yet in my own experience I must say I seemed only to find a capacity for contrition without compromise when Catholic teaching established for me a clear distinction between repentance and regret. As a Protestant the lack of any absolute absolution seemed to leave me victim of a ceaseless chain of regrets, that chewing of the cud of one's own actions that becomes itself a morbid vice. The Catholic, howsoever his self-knowledge may impress upon his mind the weakness of his resolution, knows that the will to renounce his sin that is implicit in penitence is sufficient for him to receive effective absolution which, while it cannot deflect the consequences of sin, carries the blessed succour granted to a child who knows himself forgiven by a loving parent—the succour without which peace of mind is so difficult to know. Confession offers a true catharsis that dispels regrets which readily become morally debilitating.

Another idea about confession prevalent amongst Protestants is that the relationship between priest and penitent is closely akin to that between the psychiatrist and his patient. This is not so—although demonstrably those who lack the facilities of the confessional are more likely to become the patients of psychiatrists. While a wise and understanding priest is particularly well qualified to give advice, that is not his primary concern which is the administering of a sacrament not on the strength of his personality but "as one having authority".

This brings us to an all-important distinction between the Catholic priesthood and the Presbyterian ministry. In Protestant days I often felt that there was something of an unfair judgment put upon ministers and parsons, that, while merely human themselves, they seemed to have to assume a righteousness that they probably did not feel, but without which they betrayed their position. But the priest's is an objective office, in an important sense not dependent upon him. It is a power, the apostolic succession, conferred upon him. Like holy matrimony, although it is a means to grace it is no guarantee of goodness or of adequacy in a vocation that, however, it does not leave subject to personal merit. Human nature being what it is, there are always those who fail their vocation. One out of twelve apostles failed in a terrible way: all had moments of weakness. Just as the priest is endowed with a greater potential for good, his failure is a stronger potential for evil. Protestant doctrine was the work of Catholic priests who failed in a promise that should have remained sacred for them whatever the welter of chaos and abuse in which they found themselves. We may have deep sympathy for them in the state in which they found the Church, such as we have for Catholics whose marriages are tragic and who, in human weakness that may be far from entirely bad in its motives, break their vows. But we know that those who keep their vows, at what may be agonizing cost, keep themselves more profoundly "in Christ, and him crucified". For Catholics holy orders and matrimony are primarily sacraments, not personal predilections, not therefore dependent upon feelings or wishes or merit, but going outside us, sustained by a grace beyond us, demanding a humble acceptance of the divine will that overrides intellectual or emotional enthusiasm and despair.

Perhaps, after all, it is not surprising that to an inadequate comprehension there should even seem to be something sinister about the priesthood! For there is mystery about it just as, as we are more willing to admit, if often only rather sentimentally, there is a mystery, a hidden certainty, in marriage. To Scots long brought up in the "democratic" Presbyterian tradition, with its assumption that things are best understood and resolved by the pooling of ideas, the claim of the Church to divine revelation is a formidable challenge. It is perhaps very remotely analogous to the claim of a poet to an inspired percipience that is liable to be denied to a committee. Yet, while to some degree the Church's claims must always remain the same affront to the world as were those of its Founder, there should by now be some assurance at least as to its intellectual stature in the consistency of the thought and speculation of its greatest minds, from Jerome and Augustine, Aquinas and Alphonsus, down to Newman, and in the spirituality developed by the Victorines, Thomas à Kempis (beloved of many Presbyterians), Ruysbroeck, Ignatius, John of the Cross. These are men whose work cannot be disregarded by serious theologians or thinkers of any persuasion, but we cannot say as much of the spokesmen of the Church of Scotland, much of whose writing, where it is not merely politics, is a slow retraction from an untenable position and as such often heartfelt rather than intellectually solid, and showing little enough in the way of consistent development.

Perhaps the most absurd and uncomprehending, fundamentally sentimental, suggestion is that there is something peculiarly Scottish in Presbyterianism that is not to be found in Catholicism. Certainly the national characteristics have shaped our Presbyterianism, but the Catholicism of every country receives the imprint of its people, a quality shaped by climate and race, by living conditions and history. The universality of the Church exists not in sameness but in multitudinous diversity, not flattening-out but uniting the peoples in their distinctiveness through the acceptance of truth that is above human foible. And we might well expect that the universality of true religion would require a broader basis for its full development and expression than could be afforded by one country.

In the Highlands I have lived in both Catholic and Protestant parts, and cannot feel that the religious anxiety often liable to inhibit graciousness in the Calvinist communities is in any desirable way more "Scottish" than the more general warmth and happiness of the Catholics. When times were very hard in the last century, such a man as Fr Allan MacDonald of Eriskay, labouring tirelessly amongst his people, exemplifies all that is best in the Hebrides that he loved so well and of whose spiritual freedom he wrote when it was suggested that he might seek more comfortable quarters: "I own the Isles from Barra Head to the very Butt of Lewis so far as I can walk or sail a skiff; the sea is mine to the dip of it, and all the winds come neighbourly to my door; would I change for a display of stone and mortar the mood that makes me free of all, and one and equal with the universe?"

All of the best of Presbyterian simplicity, but without any overhang of its apprehensiveness, was expressed by an old Catholic lady, a neighbour of mine, when she was receiving the last sacraments. She was ninety-two and had had a hard life of much poverty, yet she rejoiced in it all, bright-eyed making her testament, "I have had a happy life, and if ever I was unhappy it was only my own evil nature." She was one of the happiest people I ever met.

This old lady lived where she was born in an island with an indigenous Catholic population. Protestants whose families had been brought in some generations ago lived generally on the best of terms with their Catholic neighbours. Certainly such bigotry as there might be was on the Protestant side, in the persons of wives brought in from the intenser Calvinist regions, and sometimes stirred up by the strange and unwelcome intrusion of the missionaries of some English evangelical body. Once a Catholic crofter working in his hayfield was accosted by a posse of these brash enthusiasts demanding, "Have you found Jesus?" He replied with the kindly dignity of one whose forebears had not suffered the same deprivation, "I did not know that he was lost."

I remember arriving in a larger and more completely Catholic island on a holy day, not long after returning from the Continent, and, seeing the joyful faces of the people coming from Mass, suddenly knowing a wonderful sense of unity that made the lovely whitesand-fringed shores, the glistening grasses and little island hills of the Atlantic edge, a part again of greater Europe. For these people were rejoicing in the same ministration of the Universal Church that they shared with countless millions in Italy, France, in Spain and Portugal, and indeed through most of the world. It did not make them any the less Scottish.

While Irish immigration on a large scale has long ceased, and in fact for many years now has been smaller than that from England, some Catholics from other countries have come among us, from Italy and Poland and Lithuania and, since the war, the Ukraine. It would ill become Scots who have gone to help to populate so many countries, old as well as new, to resent this interchange or cavil at new blood, for the good citizen of any country is he who serves it, not he who sentimentalizes over it. A more equal numerical balance, and a growing sense of Scottish nationality amongst the descendants of the latter-day Irish in-comers, have contributed to a steady improvement in the relation-ship between Catholics and Protestants in the industrial areas. If bigotry in Scotland is still more marked amongst Protestants than Catholics, there are historical reasons for this. We usually have to learn the hard way, and the Catholics of this country, having been a minority and suffered much from intolerance in the past, have reason to have learnt abhorrence of the crass stupidity that judges not by the light of intelligence but by the darkness of prejudice. Many decent Protestants would probably be surprised to know just how much of bigotry persists amongst their own people. Its influence is always baleful, and baleful far beyond its immediate effects. It is, after all, a product of a timidity that is at least spiced with malevolence, and such fearfulness always vitiates a man's potential service to the commonweal. It is bad enough in spheres of commerce and local government: when it infects those intellectual activities that should be the source of enlightenment it is a crippling inhibition. It is not unknown in our universities, and for many years now it has had a stultifying influence upon our broadcasting, and has, by its indirect effects, reduced the Scottish Region of the B.B.C. to being the worst of the regional units, where we may well feel that it should, with the rich and still relatively autonomous material at its disposal, have been the best.

Of course Catholics are not free themselves of bigotry, sometimes appalling in its presumption and pettiness. There is even a kind of bigotry amongst those who wish to spread their faith as it were indiscriminately, to increase the total score, to sustain their own conviction. There is only one honest motive for wanting to convert other people, a sense of personal love that, with all the delicacy that love demands, wishes to give something of the utmost value to those beloved. But there is one aspect of the Catholic mentality which quite unjustly gives rise to an impression of bigotry. Whereas the Protestant who believes in private judgment may feel tentative about his beliefs, the Catholic who doubted whether his own Christian belief was the true faith would, quite simply, cease to be a Catholic. But it is not bigotry to be convinced in our beliefs. It is as feasible in religion as in every other sphere of life to be assured in our own convictions without doubting the good faith of those who do not share them. The theological expression "invincible ignorance" applied to those who in good faith remain outside the Church is sometimes mistakenly felt by Protestants to be a slur on them. Yet its use implies no suggestion of criticism whatsoever, but precisely the opposite. "Crass ignorance" is culpable ignorance: "invincible ignorance" connotes simply that while the Catholic Church is the Body of Christ in this world, the divinely-appointed means of salvation for all mankind, many can find their salvation without sharing full knowledge of the truth for which they yearn.

It is for Catholic and Protestant alike to know and to be reassured by one another that their disagreement entails no enmity of any kind. Both accept the Christian ideal, recognizing the reality of evil, man's need and potential for redemption in Christ, and the supremacy of love in the dispensation of an infinitely loving God. Both detest cruelty and dishonesty, the filth of licence and lust, the aggrandizement of power and the shabbiness of comfortable indifference. These are things that threaten the eternal lives of every one of us. They present themselves to succeeding generations under continually renewed disguises, and they have always their apologists in the framers of new philosophies and politics. Today their menace makes an imperative demand for unity between the Christian Churches. Our differences, however great they are, are not so great as the Person whom we seek to serve: the reflections that we see in the mirror of history may differ, but the cross is constant.

INDEX